What they're saying about this series and the authors...

"The West Orange Chamber of Commerce is proud to be connected with Mike O'Keefe, Scott Girard and Marc Price of **Expert Business Advice**. Their dynamic presentations, intellectual wealth, and unique insight into small business have helped numerous Chamber members take their businesses to the next level."

> Krista Compton Carter, IOM
>
> West Orange Chamber of Commerce Vice President
>
> Winter Garden, FL USA

"I've had the pleasure of working with Michael O'Keefe on many projects over the years. His ability to evaluate situations, identify competitive advantage opportunities and implement well thought-out strategic plans is second to none."

> Jim Costello
>
> Director of Project Management
>
> Marriott International Design & Construction Management

"Marc Price is a business builder! I have seen him start with a blank piece of paper and create a million dollar business for a financial education online application and service. He is a natural network builder and relationship marketer who works hard, is very creative, and who usually surpasses all objectives for sales, service, and market share growth. You want Marc on your team if your goal is to grow your brand and increase top and bottom lines."

> Mike Schiano, MA, CRHC, CPFC
>
> Information and Technology Services

MANAGING YOUR BUSINESS

CRASH COURSE for
ENTREPRENEURS

MANAGING YOUR BUSINESS

Learn What You Need in Two Hours

Scott L. Girard, Jr., Michael F. O'Keefe
and Marc A. Price

Series Editor: Scott L. Girard, Jr.

A Crash Course for Entrepreneurs—From Expert Business Advice

Starting a Business

Sales and Marketing

Managing Your Business

Business Finance Basics

Business Law Basics

Franchising

Business Plans

Time and Efficiency

International Business

Supplemental Income

Social Media

Web-Based Business

For Wouter

Contents

Foreword

ENTREPRENEURS USUALLY ARE GIFTED in the essentials of the businesses they start. But their success can't rest on that alone. They usually become jacks of all trades, gradually acquiring a working knowledge of all the facets of their businesses, including playing the role of leader and top manager.

So if you are thinking of starting a business, or have one running already, you'll understand why this book exists. If your personal strengths are in the area of business management, you'll find it a quick refresher that will help you rethink some things and learn others. If leading and managing are new challenges for you, you'll be glad you invested the two hours or so that it will take you to read it, and you'll no doubt come back for re-reads many times in the future.

You may be a one-person band, or the only manager in your company. Or, if you have a larger company, you may manage other managers. Whatever your scale of business, having a strong grounding in the thinking and practices of managers will make you a more effective leader and do-er.

When I met Scott, Mike and Marc, I knew before they told me about the 17 businesses they've collectively started that these were talented, insightful, seasoned entrepreneurs. We quickly agreed to develop the Crash Course for Entrepreneurs together.

The aim of this series is to give you high-level overviews of the critical things you need to know and do if you want to survive and thrive in this super-competitive world. Of course, there's much more to know about every topic we visit here, but we believe that what you'll read here will give you the framework for learning the rest. A Resources section and a Glossary will ensure you can ground yourself in the essentials. And the co-authors' website, www.expertbusinessadvice.com, offers expanded support for entrepreneurs that is updated daily. They pledge to get back to you with a personal reply within 24 hours, if you write to them!

Entrepreneurs vary widely in what they want to do. Your dream may be to start a very small, one-person service, perhaps doing home maintenance or day care or accounting from your home. You may have developed or discovered a high-tech breakthrough that will need years of testing and dozens or hundreds of people to bring it to market. This book sees the intrinsic value and challenges of both styles of business. It will definitely help you manage both your business and the people in it well, so you can make the most of your opportunity, whatever its scale.

Most of the chapters in this book represent the authors' collective experience and point of view, but a few are personal pieces. You'll find the initials of each author at the end of those. Here's a brief word from each of them.

I remember when I fully understood what our series of books should accomplish. Mike, Marc and I had only decided that we wanted to write a series of books for people only moderately familiar with entrepreneurship and business. Multitudes of books already exist on basic levels of business practices and procedures. We knew that writing another one of those books wouldn't really serve anyone or change anything, no matter how well written it was.

On the morning that I "got it", I was drinking coffee and reading the news; the television was on in the background. I glanced up and saw a commercial for a foreign language software program in which, instead of learning by simply repeating vocabulary, the student is culturally immersed in the language, holistically surrounded with concepts of all manner of things applicable to the subject. In short, they don't list facts and terms and call it teaching—they show the student a vast array of information, on a multitude of levels, allowing her to bathe in knowledge. I knew then that instead of presenting a bunch of facts that we think you should know about managing your business, we should take a more holistic approach and help you immerse yourself in these critical aspects of business. Our method is most effective if you read this book cover to cover, skipping nothing. If you reach a chapter and either think it doesn't address your needs, or you think you know everything there is to know about the subject, read it anyway. It'll only take a minute—that's why the chapters are not lengthy. It will enlighten and organize your thinking, either way. You'll see important concepts woven through various discussions, as they holistically fit in.

If you're hoping to read a book and immediately become the world's greatest business manager, this book isn't for you. If your goal, however, is to quickly understand and feel familiar with the basics, as your first stepping-stone to greatness, we believe that our book has no rival. I sincerely hope that this book will not only help you to successfully manage your business, but that it also gives you pleasure and satisfaction as you learn how to do it better than you ever thought you could.

Scott L. Girard, Jr.

When we sat down and decided to take on the daunting task of writing a series of books for entrepreneurs and small business owners, I cringed. I thought, "How can we ever reduce our advice and experiences to writing? And how can we cover it all—can we fit it into a book?"

Either way, we decided to get started, so each of us began drafting chapters related to our respective specialties and work experience. Only as the initiative continued did I discover a certain passion for sharing my advice in a personal way, trying to convey how it felt to plunge into running a business—to plan, execute, review, celebrate or correct, and try to do even better on the next round.

I hope that this book will capture your interest, provide valuable information, and share practical, effective techniques for your own company.

Mike F. O'Keefe

Everyone has heard the phrase "Knowledge is Power." I would have it read "Information is Power", for a couple of reasons. We live in an age of instant information about every facet of our lives. We can receive news, on-demand weather and traffic reports, sports scores, social media happenings, and stock market updates. And yet, we forget much of this information within moments of receiving it, as new reports and updates are constantly replacing the data we were just beginning to process.

Most generic information travels fast these days. On the other hand, some information is meant to stay with us for a while, if not forever. And with that in mind, Scott, Mike and I set out to write a series of books to deliver lasting, valid information for entrepreneurs and small business people.

Our passion for success in business and in life lies behind every page we write. As life-long, serial entrepreneurs, we have always taken the approach of surrounding ourselves with information, ideas and viewpoints from countless sources to support our efforts in constructing our next project. That information, when reliable and trustworthy, can and will be used over and over for repeated success.

So, in essence, information is power, when applied over time. Our series of books represents the hard work, research and application of numerous business philosophies, ideas and viewpoints. You will find rock-solid information that can be applied now... and later. It's information that can be shared, and then referred to as a refresher down the road, if needed. Our goal was to deliver business management advice that is relevant, smart and timely.

We hope these fresh, contemporary approaches will get you, and keep you, at the top of your game. The way forward begins here...

Marc A. Price

We all hope this book helps you translate the fire and drive you feel as an entrepreneur into solid successes as you manage your business, day to day. And we wish you success.

Kathe Grooms
Managing Director, Nova Vista Publishing

CHAPTER I
Leadership Basics

Leadership Styles

Which style do you use? Which ones should you learn?

BY THE TIME you decide you want to start your own business, you've already experienced virtually every style of leadership there is. You may not realize it, but you've already become one type of leader or another—you have a natural leadership style. The question now is whether the leader you *are* is the leader you want to be. And also, whether learning to use other leadership styles will pay off for you.

Parents, teachers, older siblings, bosses, police officers, military superiors—we've all had them for most of our lives. Some pulled productivity and efficiency out of us by enabling and encouraging us. A few were demanding, and that may have been just what we needed. Others were easy-going, and that did the trick. Different styles work for different types of people and in different situations.

Think for a moment—which ones worked for you? More importantly, which ones didn't work for you? As the founder of your enterprise, you are its leader. But it's not all about you—or at least it shouldn't be. You're not the one executing the work; your people are. Your job as a leader is to empower them to be productive, and sometimes that might mean trying methods that may not have worked with you in the past. But they might work with them.

Be smart about this, however. Picture a continuum stretching from accommodating to intimidating leadership styles. According to Leigh Bailey and Maureen Haben Bailey,* Accommodators need acceptance and Intimidators need control. Both styles have good and bad aspects, and both styles can be harmful if a leader puts personal needs ahead of the good of the company.

While research suggests that being overly dominant presents the greatest risk of leadership derailment, the appropriate use of a forceful leadership style is critical to a leader's success. So let's say you are mainly an accommodating leader. Should you learn to be more forceful? The answer is yes, for some situations, like when you need to firmly commit your organization to a certain change, or to deal with a challenging

---

*Leigh Bailey and Maureen Haben Bailey, *Grown-Up Leadership: The Benefits of Personal Growth for You and Your Team* (Nova Vista Pubishing, 2005).

person or situation. If you tend to be an Intimidator, you can benefit from loosening your grip and taking more risks to allow your people to learn from their successes and failures. The idea is to discover your natural style and then learn others so you can be a *versatile* leader, one who is effective in many different kinds of leadership situations.

Of course, nobody likes to be degraded or made to feel stupid or unappreciated, especially in front of others. Depending on the situation, a bit of "tough love" might work on certain employees, but be very careful with it. Think long and hard about how you're going to use it.

In my organization, when it comes to tough love, I tend to work up to it. I see difficult people as a valid leadership challenge. You can't just go around firing people—they are assets to your business and it's your responsibility to find out how to get good work from them. As you know, your leadership position makes you very visible. If you don't succeed with difficult people, you may get a reputation as a poor leader, which is the last thing you want. Nevertheless, sometimes people just don't work out, and that's life in business. That's another decision for another day.

Today, we're thinking about what type of leader you should be to get the most out of people. While taking more control has its place, here's a hint from history: Tyrannical leaders rarely last long and their dethroning is usually a painful event, so don't go too far in that direction. But doormat leaders don't get things done. It's best to recognize that each person and situation will respond best to a certain style of leadership, and to be able to be versatile enough to use the right one from moment to moment.

To this end, analyze what types of people you are dealing with and ask yourself what you can do to make them feel secure with your organization. Most need to feel motivated and guided by you.

It's always good to lead by example. If people have to work late to finish a big project, it would be good if you join them (if you're not in the way!), to show them that you are willing to go through hard times with them. If you have other obligations, come back later with some coffee or snacks.

Don't micro-manage them, however. Nothing stifles productivity like a pair of eyes constantly looking over your shoulder.

It's common for entrepreneurs to complain that with all the interruptions they get from freelancers, employees, vendors, the bank, and even their kids, they just can't get their own work done. So they close their office door to make progress. That makes sense, but don't make it a full-time habit. Try to schedule open door time—or if you can afford it, keep the door open almost all the time. People need and like to know that you are there with them.

As you think about what kind of business leader you want to be, think in specifics: consider that difficult person or that upcoming event, and ask yourself what style of leadership would work best. If you do your homework right, you will immediately be pointed in the right direction. Then just go for it and learn from your experience.

S.G.

Effective Leadership Theories

*Leaders aren't born, they're made. Here's
how to transform yourself into one.*

TO LEAD an organization successfully, you have to be more than a manager: You must also be an organizer and problem solver. You must effectively support and direct others, thinking internally, as well as handle the challenges brought on by external factors, like economic developments or new technologies. It doesn't matter how large or small your enterprise is. A lot rests on your shoulders.

Leadership theories

Among the many theories of leadership, three are intriguing and effective in practice: McGregor's Theory X and Theory Y, Action-Centered Leadership, and the Strategic Leadership Theory.

Douglas McGregor's Theory X and Theory Y were developed in the 1960s but are still commonly used. Both theories focus on motivation and on how leadership has a profound effect on employee productivity and attitude.*

Theories X and Y have been a topic of spirited debate among researchers and professionals alike for years. Theory X says that the average worker inherently dislikes work and tries to avoid it. He or she wants security, but lacks ambition. As a result, this worker must be controlled, directed and possibly threatened in order to perform well. This theory describes a leader who has control issues and is pessimistic about his team, which results in the leader taking an authoritative, iron-fisted approach.

Theory Y says that the average worker is naturally motivated to work, is very self-directed or self-controlled, seeks and accepts responsibility without reservation, and applies ambition and creativity. The potential contributions of this

*Douglas McGregor, *Management: The Human Side of Enterprise* (McGraw Hill, 1960).

type of worker are only partially used. In this view, it is the leader's responsibility to organize a team so people can work freely and to adopt a coaching approach. This theory describes a leader who has a positive view of her team and sees members as equal contributors to the organization and its goals.

Take a look at your own perceptions of your employees, and consider how they may enhance or hinder the way you manage and lead them. As with many schemas, you may find that you modify them in practice, but still, these models of two very different perceptions are worthwhile tools to guide your actions.

Developed by John Adair, the Action-Centered Leadership model focuses on what a leader has to actually do in order to make his or her team effective.** The model consists of three main activities: achieving the task, building and maintaining the team, and developing each individual within the team. For entrepreneurs who manage employees, this model is vital because a successful business rides on the shoulders of a strong team. Conversely, a weak team can destroy an otherwise solid business model.

The Strategic Leadership theory is a relatively new concept that focuses on strategy development and change.*** Everyone uses some elements of strategic leadership in their job. Professor Roger Gill argues that six components of strategic leadership include determining your strategic direction (as in writing an operations plan), developing your capabilities (as in conducting a self-evaluation on your true capabilities), and exploiting and maintaining your strengths (as in simply accentuating your positives). This theory describes everyone as a leader of sorts, with you as the top leader, creating a shared vision, linking everyone's efforts and contributions to the organization's goals, and making improvements in it.

Weaknesses of contemporary models

It's notable that many contemporary leadership models fail to address the importance of a vision for the future and a leader's need for awareness of external factors. These factors can include recognizing new trends in business, understanding cultural diversity, embracing the latest technologies, networking, and even sharing leadership roles. As an entrepreneur, you'll have to use common sense in paying attention to these equally important factors.

Influencing change and creating a culture

If your company has been around for a while, you may have already experienced the need to change significantly. Dawn Price, Regional Director for ZRS Management in Orlando, Florida has observed in a speech, "A great leader in some organizations can be more effective than the CEO." An effective leader

---

** Action-Centered Leadership and the Three Circles (image and words) are all Trademarks of Adair International Ltd.

*** Roger Gill, *The Theory and Practice of Leadership*, Second Edition (Sage, 2011).

thrives on change, identifying opportunities for it, initiating and managing it, planning to implement it, involving people who will be affected by it, and listening to people's reactions to it. None of this is easy, but it's your responsibility to steer the course.

Much of the same can be said about your role in defining or creating a corporate culture within your company. Roger Gill notes that a people-oriented corporate culture that fosters empowerment, mutual trust, and respect is more conducive to high performance than one that is not.

Personal values are another factor that influences a leader's success. Research has found that personal integrity, ambition, concern for others, loyalty and self-awareness support it. And of course, a fundamental value that cannot be ignored is proper business ethics.

All of this may seem hopelessly high-minded and a bit abstract, but as an entrepreneur you already know—or soon will learn—that the ability to translate the gleam in your eyes into a working proposition and business success starts and ends with you and your ability to engage others in making your vision a reality.

Leading a Learning Culture

*Regardless of the scope or size of your business, a
learning culture underpins sustainable success.*

IF YOU ASK TEN PEOPLE to give you the definition of *management,* you will
get as many interpretations. That's not much help to you as an entrepreneur with
a business to manage. But here's a good one: George R. Jones and Jennifer M.
George describe management as "The planning, organizing, leading and control-
ling of human and other resources to achieve organizational goals efficiently and
effectively."*

From the local entrepreneur to the largest global player in the biggest of
industries, the fundamentals of management still apply. When you are a one-person enterprise, it's a ton of hard work, but it's actually fairly simple to manage your
operation. Meetings are a matter of sitting yourself down, focusing and thinking
clearly. Planning is so often dictated by external factors that you may feel there's
no room to consider options. However, if you manage yourself well, keep on
learning, and survive long enough to expand, your organization can grow, and
new and more complex layers of management can become necessary. At that
point, even if management doesn't appeal to you, you *have* to manage more people
than just yourself. Later, you will probably be called on to manage and monitor
others in management roles.

In an expanding business, if you still run it like you did when you were on
your own, you'll pay the price. If you remain the sole source of growth, innova-
tion, responsibility and momentum, you'll limit your company's rich opportunities
for success. From the start, create a culture of learning, and you will see mush-
rooming growth.

* George R. Jones and Jennifer M. George, *Essentials of Contemporary Management*, Fifth Edition (Richard Irwin, 2012).

A corporate culture of learning

In one of my entrepreneurial projects some years ago, my consulting firm was recruited by an organization in the credit and financial literacy arena to take on a large-scale, nationwide project. This very public position required expert knowledge of the industry, vast media and public speaking skills, and managing a sizeable workforce. Looking back at both the success of the project and the organization itself, it was clear that my client's excellent management was the key factor of the organization's success. My work with them showed me the value of first-class management and became the blueprint for my own management activity.

The industry I was hired into was constantly bombarded by external change. Compliance issues, government rulings, new statistics and the status of the economy were only a few of the critical factors demanding constant attention. Managers with these responsibilities had to monitor and respond to an ever-changing landscape. They had to make independent judgments and take action on their own, with enormous consequences and serious accountability.

How was this possible? This organization had its hierarchy and decision-making processes, like most businesses. The results it achieved, however, were staggering. Its success came from its culture: *It was a learning organization*, one which empowers its managers to be creative, innovative and even self-sufficient at times. And it functioned as a team environment.

What's in this tale for you as an entrepreneur? The learning environment was present even in the organization's early existence. There was an unwritten rule: to vigorously encourage creativity through new ideas (and valid feedback when necessary), throughout the entire workforce. The place radiated fresh ideas, unique perspectives, and new strategies. This practice had another bonus: employees knew their efforts were being not only recognized, but implemented as policy. It gave them a sense of ownership and loyalty.

One example was an innovative control system feature that was suggested, designed and put into action on all products available through the organization's multiple websites. This breakthrough was a smash hit, hailed by top executives and consumers alike. Consumer confidence skyrocketed, sales took off, and high profits resulted.

So even if you are on your own, and certainly if your company has grown so that a corporate culture has started to develop, think about the massive benefits of making it a place where employees really feel able to make a difference, and pour their best work into making that happen.

M.P.

Basic Leadership Skills

As a leader, your employees aren't much without you,
but you're not much without them either.

SOME PEOPLE ARE BORN with leadership qualities—others acquire them through experience. Leadership is the ability to align and motivate a group of people so you all can achieve a common goal. The following are some qualities of an effective leader:

- Excellent listening skills. Active listening goes hand-in-hand with action and it includes effective interpretation of both verbal and nonverbal cues. Promptly reply to people's concerns. If a stalemate develops in a group, address the matter before it gets out of control. Don't expect that it will solve itself if you don't take any action. Remember as well that if a stalemate develops, is up to you as the leader to choose a solution and to stick to it.

- Impartiality. Avoid taking sides or giving special attention to particular members of a group. Don't support those who like your ideas and reject those who oppose them. Furthermore, avoid showing more concern to people who share the same background as you while opposing ones who are dissimilar in terms of beliefs, culture, life style or race.

- Respect. When conflict arises in a group, arrange a meeting with dissatisfied group members to establish a common ground for both sides. Don't suspend or expel dissenting voices. A variety of perspectives is healthy. And if people are not treated with respect, they could even decide to take legal action against you.

- Good communication skills. You must be able to express your ideas effectively. Radiate calm confidence and aim at clear, simple, actionable statements. Where necessary, use relevant examples to explain complex ideas. Adapt your speech to the needs and interest of your audience. Boring people to death is not a sign of leadership, nor is talking down to people. And when you take a significant action, ask yourself, "Who needs to know about this?" Keeping people in the loop gains their support.

- Cultural sensitivity. Sensitivity to intercultural nuances can also help in leading your group. Try to understand the cultural dynamics motivating each member. What is considered acceptable by one culture may be rejected by another, and the way one culture expresses its ideas may be foreign to the next culture. If you can identify these influences, you can bring together various cultures for a common good.

- Dedication to give and take. Communication is a two-way process of giving and receiving feedback. Don't speak nonstop, except when it's really a speech. Attune yourself to the group's mood and call for participation. Some leaders even declare that "Silence means agreement", to encourage a free flow of ideas and opinions. If you don't give the group time to respond to your statements, they will view you as domineering and start to disconnect.

- Ability to delegate. When you delegate a task, make sure your message is clear, concise, actionable, and that the outcome (a report, for example) is defined for delivery (end of day next Thursday). If you are leading a group through a series of meetings, it is smart to appoint a co-leader who can carry on with duties in case you are absent. Delegation of duty should not be done by favor, but rather on merit.

- Clear about expectations. As with delegating, making your expectations clear helps you to lead effectively. You can't expect people to read your mind. So if you ask someone to check on the competition's pricing, explain whether this information should be delivered in a formal report with graphs and charts, a phone call, or a sticky note. If you form a group to accomplish a goal, make sure the members know why they are included and what you expect them to bring to the table (even literally!).

- Flexible within reason. Neither rigidity nor wishy-washiness works in leadership. If you resist adopting valid new ideas proposed by others, you stifle creativity and may miss important breakthroughs. Good leaders never think they are the only ones with solutions, even if their experience and insight raises their odds of good judgment. Ability to change with time and openness to new thinking and action mark good leaders. And they take decisions in a timely way. Not deciding is deciding, and that frustrates others immensely.

- Accessible. You have lots to do, but if you avoid certain individuals or set yourself apart from your group by closing doors, being super busy, etc., you send a message that is certainly not leader-like.

- Humble. A leader should follow company rules he expects other group members to abide by.

- Credible. As the leader of your enterprise, you are its most visible public face. Your dealings with the banks, vendors, customers and other parties all reflect on your company. Professional, credible behavior will win respect and willingness to work with you, both inside and outside your organization.

The good news is that even if you aren't a born leader, you can polish up your leadership skills. Self-awareness and thinking about how you come off to others is a good place to start. Really building rapport and earning people's respect can then follow. Try to keep a positive, creative, adaptive and flexible attitude, and people will follow your lead.

CHAPTER II
Polishing Yourself Up

Professional Etiquette

*There are a few basic rules. Follow
them and win. Don't—and lose.*

FIRST IMPRESSIONS ARE VITAL in business. As an entrepreneur, it may take you a while to get used to being the head of your enterprise, and to act like you are. Since it's rare for someone to sit you down and run through the dos and don'ts of professional etiquette, we're going to do that now. You'll probably find a mix of news, familiar points to remember, and confirmation you're doing things right.

Basics

Aim to impress. We don't mean this in a phony way. Be buttoned down. Be well prepared, well dressed, well spoken, well behaved. When you meet with others outside your business, try to present yourself so they will end up thinking, "I bet that person gets things done!" or "That's the person I'm going to call when I need X."

Make sure that you're always on time, preferably early. That applies to showing up to meetings as well as delivering something. Many things can make you late, so plan with padding to accommodate obstacles and delays.

Lateness is just plain unprofessional. When you are late, people assume that you can't even manage yourself. With that attitude, why would they trust your business?

In growing numbers, businesses are embracing the idea that ten minutes early is "on time", so if you walk into a meeting the moment it's scheduled to start, you're late. If you arrive slightly early, you can get a feel for the atmosphere and environment, and take a moment to chat with others or review your meeting notes. Get your materials ready, pour yourself something, and collect your thoughts.

Meetings

Since you started your business, it's natural that you have a lot to say about it. But try to develop a habit of doing twice as much listening as you do talking in meetings. You *will* learn more and when you do speak, others are more likely to listen. Setting a good example will also encourage your team to be active listeners and you'll all get more done.

Be aware that as the business's founder, people watch you closely; don't slouch or display body language that suggests that you are tired, bored or disinterested.

Phones

Cell phone abuse is widespread, but that doesn't mean it's okay to do bad things. In a business setting (and that includes meals), do not use your phone without permission of the people you are with. It's that simple. Anything else says, "I don't respect you."

If it's an emergency and you need to be silently communicating, or you're expecting a genuinely important call, excuse yourself beforehand and explain the situation, particularly to the leader of a meeting. If your call comes in, excuse yourself unobtrusively and leave the group to take it. When you return to the meeting, apologize for the interruption (unless that interrupts the meeting more!).

Silence your phone whenever that's appropriate. Some people turn their phones off entirely when they are doing business. And they survive! It wasn't so long ago that we didn't have phones attached to us—remember?

When you reach someone's voicemail, be prepared with a concise message, not longer than a minute. State your name and message clearly, and wrap up with your name and phone number. It's good to repeat that number too.

Email

Your email habits also impact your professional image. When writing to someone you haven't met, use Mr., Mrs. or Ms., unless you are absolutely sure first names are appropriate. You can always get informal on the second exchange.

Never send work-related emails from your personal email account. It looks sloppy and could cause your message to get caught in a spam filter. Likewise, avoid juvenile-looking things like smiley faces or strings of exclamation points!!!!!

In a message to a new contact, introduce yourself first and, if the recipient is a referral from a mutual colleague, let the recipient know how you know her. State your action and sign off. Be sure to include your signature block with complete details (your name, title, company coordinates, email and street addresses, phones, website, etc.).

Finally, if you need to send the recipient an attachment, you might want to get his (or his receptionist's or assistant's) permission before you send it. An effective opening then can read, "Dear Mr. Hill, I spoke with [name]today and she suggested I send you this note, along with an attachment that describes our services."

Keep your message concise and to the point. Spell check everything automatically.

We use the BLUF method, which stands for Bottom-Line-Up-Front. It goes something like this:

> Dear Mr. Green,
> It was a pleasure to meet you last week at the home builders' convention.
> I'm writing, as promised, to set an appointment with your team to demonstrate our new water-resistant wood stain at your office.
> I am available all day Tuesday and Thursday, 23 and 25 June. Could you please pick a time that's convenient for you and get back to me?
> I'm looking forward to our meeting.
> Yours truly,
> [Your name and signature block.]

As the leader of your enterprise your habits will tend to set the standard for employees. It pays to model the best etiquette you can and to coach your team so they can improve where necessary. With a little attention and effort, these points of etiquette can easily become habits. Their impact point by point is not necessarily huge, but taken together, they will give you a solid, professional image that will be a great support to your business's success.

Common Writing and Speaking Mistakes

Nobody's perfect. But most common mistakes are completely avoidable with a bit of extra knowledge and practice.

IT STINGS A BIT when someone corrects your speech or writing. It's embarrassing to be wrong, and embarrassing to have it pointed out.

But when you think about it objectively, you face lots of challenges in other areas as an entrepreneur, and you probably like learning new things that make your business more successful. So why not be open to improving how you express yourself? Here are some tips and some common errors to avoid. All you have to do is address any weak spots you notice.

Correct speaking and writing is expected in business today, even though language skills are not always taught effectively in some schools. If you can't communicate intelligently and professionally, it damages your image. And if your team lacks polish, that indirectly reflects badly on you. If you say that you like to eat "*eye-talian*" food, it's not the end of the world, but people notice and your overall credibility suffers.

Imagine you are interviewing a young man for a job in your business and he says, "I want to work here because *supposably* this is a great place to work." If you hire him, give him this chapter to read. Or hire someone with better language skills.

"So what?", you may say. "Everybody says '*towards*' and writes *alright*." The question is this: Do you want to be wrong like "everybody", or do you want to be right? You work hard to make sure your product or service is better than the competition's. So take charge of your verbal skills to make sure they don't undercut everything else you do.

Here's a tip: put an X in the boxes next to any errors you tend to make. Then each day, pick one of them and try to use the correct form several times in both your speaking and writing. With practice the correct form will become habit. And you'll be sure your language skills are up there with the best.

Commonly misused words

- ☐ **Accept, Except:** *Accept* means to receive, while *except* means to exclude.

- ☐ **Adverse, Averse:** *Adverse* means difficult, *averse* means having a strong feeling against (like an aversion).

- ☐ **Affect, effect**: *Affect* usually means to alter; an *effect* is a result.

- ☐ **Allusion, Illusion:** An *allusion* is an indirect reference. An *illusion* is a misconception or false impression. "Did you catch my *allusion* to Edgar Allan Poe? The magician didn't actually saw the girl in half; it was simply an optical *illusion*."

- ☐ **Alright:** This just isn't a word. You should use *all right*.

- ☐ **Ask, Ax:** *Ask* is a verb meaning to verbally make a query, while an *ax* is a tool used by a lumberjack to cut down trees. If you say "I ax him to pay", it sounds almost the same as "I asked him to pay", but the difference will make you sound extremely unprofessional.

- ☐ **Assure, Ensure, Insure:** *Assure* means to guarantee, *Ensure* means to make sure, and *Insure* should only be used when talking about insurance.

- ☐ **Capital, Capitol:** *Capital* refers to a city that's a center of government, and also to wealth or resources. A *capitol* is a building where lawmakers meet. Canberra is the *capital* of Australia. Entrepreneurs need *capital* to fund start-up costs. The US *capitol* houses the Senate and House of Representatives.

- ☐ **Climactic, Climatic:** *Climactic* is derived from *climax*, the point of greatest intensity in a series or progression of events. *Climatic* is derived from *climate*; it refers to meteorological conditions. The *climactic* scene in the film was very bloody. Severe *climatic* conditions include droughts and hurricanes.

- ☐ **Compliment, Complement:** A *compliment* is praise, to *complement* is to go well with something else or balance something out.

- ☐ **Componentry:** This one is relatively uncommon, unless you work in fabrication or engineering. Often mistaken around the shop, *com-*

ponentry is just a churched-up (and completely incorrect) way to say *components.* Very similar to this engineering misnomer is *schematical,* as in *schematical* drawings. Just say *schematics* or *schematic drawings* and you'll be in the right.

- ☐ **Could of:** When you think about it, this doesn't even make sense. It comes from misspelling *could have,* or *could've.*

- ☐ **Discreet, Discrete:** *Discreet* is to be careful, *Discrete* means distinct.

- ☐ **Elicit, Illicit:** *Elicit* is a verb meaning to bring out or to evoke. *Illicit* is an adjective meaning unlawful. The detective was unable to *elicit* information from the locals about *illicit* drug trafficking.

- ☐ **Emigrate from, Immigrate to:** *Emigrate* means to leave one country or region to settle in another. *Immigrate* means to enter another country and reside there. In 1870, my great-grandfather *emigrated* from France. Many Mexicans *immigrate* to the United States to find work.

- ☐ **Farther, Further:** *Farther* refers to distance, *further* means more.

- ☐ **Foreword, Forward:** A *Foreword* is the beginning of a book; *forward* is a direction and the opposite of backward (also, it never ends in *s*).

- ☐ **i.e., e.g.,:** In Latin *i.e.* means "that is", while *e.g.* means "for example." Both have two periods and a comma when you write them: He packed his meerschaum, *i.e.,* his clay pipe. She is allergic to root vegetables, *e.g.,* beets.

- ☐ **Its, It's:** *Its* is possessive, like *his* or *her.* *It's* is short for *it is.*

- ☐ **Labtop, Laptop:** *Labtop* is not a word. The computer sits on your lap, not your lab—even if you're a scientist.

- ☐ **Like:** Don't say *like* fifteen times in a sentence. *Like* is not a placeholder—something you needlessly say to fill up space when you can't think of the right word fast enough.

- ☐ **Loose, Lose:** *Loose* is the opposite of tight, *lose* is the opposite of win.

- ☐ **No, Know:** *No* is the opposite of yes. *Know* refers to something you've learned. *Know* when to say *no.*

- ☐ **Nuclear, Nucular:** *Nucular* is a common mispronunciation, famously used by Jimmy Carter, ex-president of the US, who earlier worked in the US's *nuclear* submarine program. The trick to getting it right is to say the word exactly as it's written: "*New*-Clee-Err".

- ☐ **Precede, Proceed:** Something *precedes* if it comes first. To *proceed* is to carry on, go ahead, or continue, especially after a pause.

- ☐ **Principle, Principal:** *Principal* is a noun meaning the head of a school or an organization, or a sum of money. *Principle* is a noun meaning a basic truth or law. The *principal* taught us many vital life *principles*.

- ☐ **Realtor, reelator:** A realtor sells real estate. You won't see *reelator* in writing, but it's a common mispronunciation of *realtor*.

- ☐ **Supposedly, supposably:** *Supposedly* could be the most mispronounced word in the English-speaking world. We've all heard it: *supposably*.

- ☐ **Than, Then:** *Than* is used for comparisons, *then* means it came next. I like steak more *than* fish. We went to dinner, *then* to a movie.

- ☐ **There, Their, They're:** *There* is a place, *their* is something that belongs to them, *they're* is short for *they are*. *There* are two monsters in *their* closet and *they're* scaring the kids to death!

- ☐ **To, Two, Too:** *Two* is a number, *too* means also, *to* is used with verbs (going to). We have *two* cats. I like cats, *too*! Let's go *to* the pet store and buy them some catnip.

- ☐ **Weather, Whether:** *Weather* is what the meteorologists predict, *whether* is used when making a choice. I don't know *whether* or not to go out in this terrible *weather*.

- ☐ **Whose, Who's:** *Whose* is possessive, *who's* is short for *who is*.

- ☐ **Your, You're:** *Your* points to something that belongs to you, *you're* is short for *you are*.

Words that don't sound alike but confuse us anyway

- ☐ **Lie, Lay:** This one's a little tricky. *Lie* means to say something that's not true, or to recline or rest on a surface. The principal parts for the resting sense are *lie, lay, lain*. The verb *lay*, in the present tense, has a lot of meanings, but to put or place something flat is what we focus on here. Its principal parts are *lay, laid, laid*. Think of it like this: *I lie down when I am tired. Lay your cards on the table.*

- ☐ **Less, Fewer:** In general, use *less* if it describes something that doesn't have individual items (called group nouns). *Less water, less time, less pain, less hope.* Water and time are tricky because you can count water in gallons and time in seconds. If your focus is the count, say *fewer seconds of* *time* or *fewer gallons of water*. If you can count the number of something (count nouns), say *fewer*. All those store signs saying "ten items or less" are just plain wrong: It should be "ten items or fewer." *Fewer children, fewer questions, fewer cars*. British English adds a further complication here because it views nouns like *team* as a plural, so the correct British usage is "the team are ready for the game."

- ☐ **Set, Sit:** *Set* means to put or to place. Its principal parts are *set, set, set*. *Sit* simply means to be seated. Its principal parts are *sit, sat, sat*. He *set* the flower pot by the window. The dog *sat* by the door all day.

- ☐ **Who, Which, That:** Do not use *which* to refer to people. Use *who* instead. *That*, though generally used to refer to things, may be used to refer to a group. I just saw a boy *who* was wearing a pirate costume. Where is the magazine *that* I was reading? I have to go to English next, *which* is my hardest class.

- ☐ **Good, Well:** Someone asks, "Good morning; how are you?" If you say, "I'm doing good", you're incorrect. Unless you plan on spending your day saving the world or doing charitable favors for people, you are doing *well*. *Good* is for things, *well* is for actions.

Problem phrases:

- ☐ **Cease and desist:** Not *cease and assist*. Same thing, a scrambling of sounds. *Cease and desist* means to absolutely stop, in legal jargon. Use *stop* if you can.

- ☐ **Couldn't care less, could care less:** Think of the literal meanings of the words and you won't say "I could care less" . Your point is that you care so little that it's not possible to care any less.

- ☐ **For all intents and purposes, For all intensive purposes:** Don't use the second phrase. It's just a scrambling of the sounds of the correct form, the first phrase here.

- ☐ **Irregardless:** *Irregardless* isn't a real word—it's considered wrong because of the double negative elements *ir-* and *-less*. Use *regardless*.

- ☐ **Supposed to:** Do not omit the *d*. *Suppose to* is incorrect.

- ☐ **Toward, Anyway:** There is no *s* at the end of these words. Although very commonly used, *towards* and *anyways* are incorrect.

- ☐ **Used to:** Same as above. Do not write *use to* if you are talking about things routinely done in the past. Write *used to*.

We'll close with a couple of additional tips that will boost your credibility through your language skills. It may seem obvious, but if you don't know much about a topic, it's best not to bluff. You run the risk of annoying everyone, or worse, getting called out by someone who actually does know about the subject. And if you are a habitual bluffer, your audience will start automatically discounting what you say—even when you actually know something.

Also, if you want to be listened to when you speak, do your best to limit *ummm, aaah, errr,* and *like.* It's annoying, and it makes you sound disorganized, nervous, or not very smart when you use these noises to fill gaps.

Instead, use a silent pause. If you need a moment to collect your thoughts, simply stop talking for a moment, even in the middle of a sentence. It's clear to everyone that you're not finished speaking, and the pause can actually get day-dreamers back to focusing on you. Also, the pause makes what follows seem a little more important. Don't overuse this, as its power comes from its surprise effect. And be aware that a silent pause may backfire on a conference call—someone may jump in to speak, or people may think you've dropped your phone line (or fallen asleep mid-sentence!).

All these tips and tricks will polish up your professional image. When you speak or write in business, it is the quality of what you say *and* how you say it that matters.

Confident or Cocky?

In business, it can mean the difference between life and death.

EVEN IF YOURS IS A TINY COMPANY, you realize how important it is to work well with other people. Thus, the way you behave and treat others is important to your success as an individual and leader of a your business team, not to mention the success of your enterprise.

Growing up, it was clear who the "cool kids" or "in crowd" were. Did you ever wonder why they were so likable? Sure, they may have been attractive, but chances are, their appeal was due to their charisma and self-confidence. You know plenty of people who aren't the best looking, but are master sellers and moguls in business, because their self-confidence makes things happen for them. But they also don't cross the line into cockiness, which is very disagreeable trait.

People express their dislike of cockiness and arrogance quite readily. You might have started your business because you actually *are* the best at what you do. So, if you are the best, how can you maintain your confidence and inspire your team without being seen as cocky? The short answer is to blend confidence with kindness and humility.

Put yourself in your teammates' shoes. Chances are, they know you're the best (or try really hard to be), and this can sometimes cause a bit of jealousy or competitiveness, especially in people who have similar skills. There's no point in reining in your confidence, though, because confidence can motivate. Be as confident as you want, but mix it with an appropriate level of kindness and humility. That should win the support of your team.

Generally, leaders who go out of their way to say good morning or ask a colleague if they can help with anything come off as confident. These people take control of the situation by initiating contact, and their confidence and kindness engages and attracts others. One extremely successful entrepreneur we know spends the first hour of every workday strolling through the office and warehouse with a cup of coffee. In the course of a week he'll have had one or more brief chats with every one of the 100 people in his organization. In those chats he asks Tom how he is coming along with the new web page, then he might ask Sarah if she's happy with the new product label, and he'll check in with Matt to see how much sleep he's getting with that new baby in the house. The employees value these check-ins because they can bring up problems and solutions informally or and set a time for a later meeting. Via this routine, the leader keeps his finger on the pulse of his company and subtly keeps everyone on track and reassured.

Another way to generate confidence is to not lose your temper or composure in a crisis. This might take practice. By staying calm, you can calm others. People will appreciate your strength and the composure you encourage in them, too.

The bottom line is that businesses are political arenas. If people like you, they generally won't oppose you; and if they like you for the right reasons, they will support you. Your sincere connections with them pay back in many ways.

CHAPTER III

Employee Management

The Bossy Boss: A Play in Three Acts

As told by a formerly bossy boss.

HERE'S A LITTLE PLAY that comes from a real-life experience.

SETTING THE STAGE: Your new, small business has finally grown to the point where you can hire people and become a real boss. You believe in your organization's mission and plan to grow it long-term. You love your business and will do anything for it; not just for you, but also for your new employees. In short, you feel like you are in a position to be the perfect boss.

ACT ONE: You've hired your first project team and want to get to know them better and share your leadership philosophy and mission statement with them (this assumes you have one—some new leaders take a year or so to develop one). Your team is as diverse as it can be. On it are people both older and younger than you; some have less experience in the industry and some have a little more. Because you care so much about the company's success, you firmly tell them how *your* team will be run and that, as their leader, *you* will be the one making all the major decisions. From that point on, no one on the team says anything.

The Plot Thickens

ACT TWO: As days go by, you work your team to the bone. Under threat of being fired, they come in early and leave late—well beyond the scope of the hours you hired them to work. Instead of encouragement, you issue threats. You want to impose your belief system on them by force. (It works in an Army boot camp, right?) When anyone smiles or laughs, you scowl and tell them to get back to work. You comment sarcastically that perhaps one of the smilers would have more fun at home, looking for a new job.

On the day of a big presentation to a new client, a team member who took the presentation materials home to give it its final touches gets in a car accident on the way to work. While his injuries are not life-threatening, he can't come to work for some time, and the presentation must be rescheduled.

Instead of showing concern for your team member, you openly criticize him, in front of the other team members, for derailing the presentation. Later, you sit in your new, big office with your desk and your window and your painting and your potted plant, and wonder why the other members of your team don't share your passion for loyally delivering for *your* company.

Two days later, it's time for your rescheduled presentation. You wait in the conference room for your team to arrive and set up. Five minutes before the meeting is scheduled to begin, your client enters the empty room. Before she can speak, you apologize, saying you don't know where your team is and that you will explain the value of punctuality to them after the presentation. Unfortunately, no one at all shows up. Your team got together and agreed that none of them need any more of your abuse, so they quit. All of them.

The Climax!

ACT THREE: Luckily, your client, another small business owner (and a really good boss) knows that your heart is in the right place and that all new leaders need leadership guidance. Unlike racehorses, new leaders spring out of the gate and run in all different directions. And so far, you have been running in the wrong direction. Your client agrees to come back in two weeks after you've hired all your employees back, hopefully to work in a more positive environment.

THE MORAL OF THE PLAY: Your client understands the value of open, balanced, two-way interaction. If one person is always pulling rank and making all of the decisions, then why is there even a team? She also believes that if you treat your employees right, they'll treat you right. If they need a little more work or time to finish a project (which is common), they will notice if you are there, too, suffering through it with them.

Lead your team by setting an example, not strong-arming them. As a business owner, you must recognize that your employees are *not* your slaves. They get work done. They can also be your 2nd, 3rd, 4th, 5th, 6th, 7th and 8th opinion on a given issue or decision. They are your human resources, and you'd be smart to treat them with respect, courtesy and appreciation.

Always remember that your employees are people, just like you. They are not perfect, they have their own challenges outside of work, and they typically won't have the expertise and comprehensive understanding of the industry you have. That's why it's up to you to foster a positive work environment for them in order to maximize learning and productivity. It's all about results, and an unhappy or abused team simply won't produce them.

The End
Roll Credits

S.G.

Establishing Goals for Your Employees

*Like stepping stones in a river, establishing
goals will guide your employees toward the
right destination without upset.*

AS AN ENTREPRENEUR, it is important to foster a sense of purpose and direction among the people in your company. One way of doing this is by establishing goals. When people have goals, they are more likely to feel motivated in their work.

But first, you must first define the goals you have in mind for your business as a whole—ideally in the short, medium and longer term. For the sake of brevity, we'll take just a short-term view. You can extrapolate how longer term goal-setting would work. Let's look at an example.

Suppose it's November and you want your sales to grow by 50 percent next year. What goals can you set for the company that will support this company goal?

1. You need to develop and produce a catalog to sell from by the end of January.

2. You need to acquire 40 new customers. Say you add 10 per quarter.

3. You need one new product release by the end of March, so you'll have sales from it for the last three quarters.

Okay, now bring in the troops. Plan a meeting in which you set out your overall company goal (50 percent growth) and the three sub-goals that support it. In this phase, you should be a directive leader, but you also need to inspire your team about your vision.

Encourage discussion and questions so the goals are crystal clear for everyone. Now ask each person to identify about three to five personal goals that will support the overall goals.

Your marketing group will have specific tasks to get done in order to get that catalog out. Maybe one of them needs to learn a new software program to make the layout process go faster. There's one goal, and for that person, it makes sense because it directly supports the goals above it in the goal hierarchy.

Your sales team no doubt will focus on the second goal, getting 40 new customers, 10 per quarter, next year. Should they buy prospect lists and do a tele-marketing blitz, or attend a trade show in the first quarter? Sometimes there will be healthy disagreement as to what actions will achieve goals best, and therefore which ones better support the ones above them. But as you can see, involving your staff in establishing their own goals will give them a sense of ownership and commitment. Conversely, if you issue goals from on high, you risk getting push-back, resentment and apathy.

Plan meetings with either key leaders or whole teams, as appropriate, to guide them in brainstorming ideas about the goals that they should set for themselves. Make sure you listen to all their suggestions, always asking how a given goal ties into the larger company goal. In theory, why would anybody do *anything* that doesn't support the goals?

Of course, as the final decision-maker, you may have to reshape or reject some ideas, but the give and take will be productive if everyone focuses on how to achieve those over-arching goals. Eventually each employee will have several specific, measurable goals for the year and they will see how each one ties to the bigger picture.

Don't stop when you finally have everybody's goals worked out. During the course of the year, it's important to monitor progress and to make adjustments as needed to keep on course. Viewed in this way, each person's performance gains a reason for being and a definite direction, and this can really spark performance. People usually feel great satisfaction in accomplishing their goals, but also in seeing how their personal contributions move the whole company forward.

This emphasis on performance toward a goal is much more positive than the old-fashioned "Let's sit down and see how you've performed this year" scenario. If someone is not performing or is missing a goal that supports the key ones, you don't have to explain how that hurts the company's progress overall.

Listen carefully in these discussions. There could be hidden reasons why someone isn't going to hit a target, and it's your responsibility to remove as many obstacles as possible.

With time, people get better and better at goal setting. If you insist that goals be SMART (Simple, Measurable, Attainable, Realistic and Timely), you will define excellent goals from the start. The key is the linkage between each level of goals and all the others.

Healthy Internal Debate and Competition

*Intelligent people disagree. As a leader, how do
you help them work productively together?*

A BIT OF HEALTHY DEBATE, and sometimes, even more than a bit, is one
sign of a group that can really produce results. However, there are risks and pit-
falls you need to spot and steer around as you encourage people to speak up.

Healthy debate—the free exchange of ideas with the intent of arriving at
the best possible outcome—both releases and creates energy. Sullen compliance,
gossip, behind-the-back griping or ill-intended input is unhealthy both for the
people doing it and for your company. If it gets out of hand, it can debilitate the
rest of a well-intending team.

Domination and passivity

Think for a moment of your company as a wolf pack. The dominant Alphas
suppress or intimidate the less aggressive, more compliant Beta people, perhaps
from natural leadership skills, but sometimes because they need to feel like they
are the best in the room and they get that feeling when bullying others. The Betas
may feel threatened by the Alphas or may secretly dismiss them, but either way
they will tend to withdraw and shut down in self-defense. Now you face a "pack"
that's only getting the benefit of Alpha talk and thought, with undercurrents of
resentment or apathy swirling beneath in the Beta's minds. The result: disengage-
ment, low productivity, and growing disrespect for you, as the top Alpha, for
tolerating this imbalance.

Your challenge is to redirect the Alphas so they treat Betas with respect and
give them time to speak. You also must redirect the Betas, encouraging them to
move out of their silent comfort zones and push back (with your support) against
Alpha dominance. This coaching is best done one-on-one, probably repeatedly,

with a lot of neutral patience. Emphasize to everyone, Alpha or Beta, that you expect everyone to work *and contribute* as a team.

If an Alpha resists change, you may have to say something like this. "I appreciate your input. You are good on task, but you are not good at something we also expect here: professional teamwork. And you are creating problems: Others are not functioning at their best because they feel defensive when you are dominant or aggressive toward them." The Alpha will notice that you admit that she is "good on task", yet hear your need for her to become a better team player.

If a Beta doesn't start contributing (and you know she has good ideas), you may need to say something like this. "You say you feel like Hans doesn't respect you. Your silence in meetings invites people to think less of you, and then they treat you with less respect than you deserve. Take pride in yourself and show that a bit by speaking up. You do your tasks well. We need your input so we can do our very best as a team. In meetings, if I ask you what you think, I expect you to speak up, not shrug and smile. Do you think you can do that?"

Then in group situations, make sure you invite the Betas to speak, and don't hesitate to shorten the talk time of the Alphas. Remind the group that silence as well as too much talk are no help in achieving your goals.

Internal competition

Here's one approach: Ensure that you don't foster a work environment that rewards internally focused competition. It's fine to award "top seller" prizes, but consider keeping the participants' sales tally private, posting only the *team's* total progress toward your sales goal. Announce only who won, not the winner's total, at the end of the competition. Even if it wasn't a photo finish, imply that it was. This way, while the competition is going on, people won't worry about what their fellow employees are doing; instead, they will focus on doing the best they can. The Betas won't be threatened by the Alphas' in-your-face attitude, and the Alphas will get their beloved competition.

If you sense, however, that you aren't dealing with an Alpha-Beta split in your sales team, then sharing the individual sales results can spur an even more intense competition. Just be aware that this approach is much more likely to spin out of control, since selling is such a complex process and combines personal effort and skill with many external factors.

Here's another real-world scenario: You have two people who work great alone but refuse to work together because they dislike each other. You feel like firing both. Should you? NO! Well, not right away, at least. There are a few tactics you can try with which I have had success in the past.

Sometimes, when two Alphas have to work closely together, it doesn't go well because they are competing against each other instead of focusing on their task or goal. We see this very often in sales or marketing teams. The salespeople want to have the highest numbers and the marketers want to be the most creative. With such intense internal competition and maybe even animosity going on behind the scenes, how can anything get done? The short answer: It can't. And you can't choose Alpha A to be the boss of Alpha B, because B will shut down and say something to himself like, "Well if she's the best, then why do I even try?"

A little-known reality in business is that Alphas perform so well because they are extremely emotionally-driven people. Their emotions are so strong and they crave being the best so badly that they will practically do anything to win. When they feel rejected, they almost always shut down. The bigger they are, the harder they fall.

So what's the solution? How do you get them work together? The answer is laughably simple: Give them a *common* goal. Seriously. They already have a common desire (to be better than everyone else, but especially the other Alpha), so force them to rely on each other to be super successful. If they are your two best marketers, put them on a project and assign one the slogan, and the other the graphic. Tell them that when they make the final presentation, they have to do it together. Make it clear, however, that if one fails to produce something of quality, the other fails for not helping. Both of their egos will be on the line for the whole of their output. So in order to create the best slogan and graphic, they will just have to figure it out together. (If you want to be really tricky, you can assign the slogan to the Alpha who you is better at graphics, and the graphic to the Alpha who is better at slogans. They won't be able to avoid helping the other, because they are driven to be the best!)

The psychology behind this is that their "Alpha-ness" will kick in and they will care more about delivering a stellar product (since it will have their name on it) than they will care about competing with the other Alpha. Typically, somewhere along the way, they will realize how much they actually have in common. Over time they probably will develop, if not a friendship, at least a mutual respect for one another. Their former perception of each other as a threat that could keep them from being *the* best may fade away.

As an entrepreneur, particularly in your start-up phase, you must ensure that your team functions as a well-oiled machine. Your customers and the bank don't care what kind of internal cohesion problems you're having. All they ultimately want from you is quality products and services and positive results. Emphasizing common goals is a proven technique for turning negative competition into successful cooperation. Allowing two Alphas fight to the death does not qualify as good leadership!

In the end, you may have to look this philosophically and with a tough hide. If you force two people who don't work well together to work as a team, one could immediately quit (which solves your dispute but cuts into your talent pool), or more likely, they both will just think you're nuts, forcing them to work together. That shared opinion *could* be the first step to developing cohesion between them!

S.G.

Presenting Problems with Solutions

*The only thing worse than a problem
is a problem without a solution.*

IF YOU CAN MAKE ONE THING CLEAR in your enterprise, you can transform it overnight.

If you have any employees at all, make every one of them responsible for proposing the solution they favor when they report a problem.

It's that easy.

If, like so many entrepreneurs, you started your business and played all of its different roles yourself, you know it through and through. As your business expands, you bring in extra hands, and before long you have departments and managers.

Ideally, you have delegated considerable responsibility to every one of your employees. They treat their areas with an attitude of responsibility and ownership. They are *the* company expert and achieve the best possible results for their business area. But in reality you have may have young, inexperienced workers; workers who are in new roles, still learning the ropes; and a certain number of timid types who may not feel comfortable with responsibility.

Every day, when a problem or question comes up, your employees make a choice. If they can resolve the issues, they will. When they need approval and input from others, they often carefully lay out the issue and then sit back, waiting for others to start coming up with answers.

It's up to you as the leader and founder of your business to make it clear that that's not how your team operates. Every problem or question must arrive with the issue owner's best guess for a solution. In practice, this may mean that you say to an issue owner, "Thank you for bringing this up. Please come back in two hours with what you think we should do." It won't take too many variations on this theme to get your team into a pro-active problem-solving habit.

Sometimes you may have to bite your tongue because the solution is crystal clear to you, thanks to your experience. But ask yourself: How else will this employee ever gain that experience if you keep jumping in with answers?

Of course, complex and high-stake issues call for group work and creative problem-solving collaboration. That's a different situation. As is the rare situation that has literally everyone stumped. But for the garden variety problems that arise day to day, your people can and should take ownership and free time and energy for leaders to work at those complex levels.

It's natural that you'll worry about the risks of this set-up, and you and others need to invest a certain amount of teaching and coaching to equip people to define problems and work out solutions. But if you do, you'll avoid the traps of micro-management that creates a culture of mediocre performance with limited ability to execute.

So hold a company-wide meeting or some smaller group ones, explain the way this will work, clarify your expectations, and get everyone moving forward in every aspect of your business. The great thing is that when it becomes your corporate culture, things can really move along fast.

Fostering a Productive Work Environment

*Getting consistent high performance
is an art. How skilled are you?*

MOTIVATING EMPLOYEES can sometimes be an uphill battle, especially if you employ people from the younger generations (though not always), or if the work your employees do is boring, monotonous, or otherwise unpleasant. It's human nature to avoid the unpleasant, so as their boss, it's up to you to motivate them into performing well.

Punctuality can be a really frustrating issue for employers. If you live in an area that has troublesome traffic conditions or bad weather for several months of the year, it can be hard or may seem a little harsh to harp on your employees about showing up to work exactly on time. Look at it this way, though: Did you get to work on time? If you can, why can't they? If five employees show up ten minutes late, five days a week, and if they each make $15 per hour, you've just paid out $63 for literally nothing. Perhaps $63 doesn't seem like a lot, but that's $250 per month, or $3,000 per year; and that's just for five people, ten minutes late each!

The moral: Either they can learn to get there early, or other arrangements should be made. Why should you pay out-of-pocket for your employees' punctuality failures, especially when you managed to get there on time, yourself? The reality is that it's not so much about the money as it is about the attitude. While money is important, if you allow your employees to cut corners one way, they're going to think it's okay to do it all the time. I can assure you that if you want to stay in business in this economy, that's not the type of environment you want to foster, especially on *your* budget. Below are a few ideas to get the most out of your employees while they're at the office.

Encourage 10-minute breaks. The key here isn't in the number of minutes. Five or fifteen minutes does the job, too. This idea might seem contradictory to what I just said about punctuality, but another performance motivator to take into consideration is boredom and fatigue.

A quick stretch or scheduled break times to refill a coffee cup or chat with co-workers will work wonders on your employees' focus and productivity. Remember, you control their hours and pay scale, so adjust both of these so that the company doesn't lose money from this. Six ten-minute breaks per day equates to an hour of paid time, so factor this in when running the annual numbers on how many employees you can afford to employ, or figuring how productive your team has been.

Another option is a simple punch clock. Pay your workers for the exact time that they are actually working. This might seem old fashioned, but the concept still holds true, today. Tell your employees that it benefits them because they will be fairly compensated for the hard work that they put in. They can't really argue with that.

Block non work-related websites during work hours. This will benefit you in multiple ways. For one thing, it will keep your employees off of Facebook and ESPN.com while they are supposed to be working. But it will also free up all the bandwidth they are eating up, allowing everyone else who is using the Internet for work to be more productive. You can block such sites through a simple adjustment to your network's firewall settings.

Think outside the job description. Sometimes, all anyone needs to jump-start their performance is an adjustment in responsibilities. As a boss, you can't play the cup game with your employees' tasks, but getting creative and engaging your employees' talents could pay dividends for you. Here's where knowing your employees personally really pays off.

Don't be afraid to reward positive performance. Occasionally, employers are hesitant to reward positive performance because they don't want to be accused of favoritism or prejudicial activity. But consider: If you have an employee who is setting an example, working at 110 percent, and really contributing to your company's success, I think that by not rewarding them, *you* are setting a bad example. Don't be afraid of giving credit where credit is due; if objections arise, cite your rewarded employees' positive performance as the justification. Just ensure that if you reward one employee for excellent performance, you reward everyone who delivers commensurate performance equally.

Set a good example yourself. Remember that as the leader, you are essentially responsible for everything your organization does or fails to do. It's hard to campaign against negative performance when you don't perform yourself. Your employees look up to you. If you choose to play a passive role or cut yourself too much slack, be prepared for the consequences. I can tell you from experience that if you have an office at your company and seldom use it, your employees won't respond well. If you feel like you've done your time at the helm and want to take a more inactive role, that's your prerogative. Just ensure that *someone* is there, running the show and monitoring performance.

S.G.

Ensuring Top-Quality Work

Ever frustrated by poor performers? A simple conversation can turn things around.

HERE'S A COMMON problem: Some of the people who work for you are either lazy or they think they're smarter than you. They cut corners and think you don't know about it. They cleverly cover their bases and have an excuse for everything. You think of firing them, but they do just enough real work to make you feel guilty about pursuing that option. Yet, it frustrates you because you pay them, they owe you good work, and you know they can do better.

As we've said, the market doesn't want to hear about your problem; it just wants your company to perform and deliver. If only you could find a way to control these team members and motivate them to care as much about their performance as you do!

"Big deal. The economy's in the tank, there are other people eager to work here, so I should just fire them." If this is your first thought, I suggest you reconsider. Typically, a high turnover rate indicates poor management, in this case yours. Firing the laggards is just short-term thinking.

Have you ever been to a restaurant whose staff all seemed unhappy and lost? It's probably because *everyone* started working there last week and they neither know each other, nor know how to work together. How well can they work together, thinking that they will probably lose their job next week because of something stupid someone else did anyway? It's not a pretty picture.

Although your employees may seem like they don't listen to you and are cutting corners to get the job done as quickly as possible, I'm ready to bet that they don't actually know what their job is. They don't know what they are supposed to be doing. (It's either that, or they just don't like you. Don't laugh: If your subordinates don't like working for you, they will go through the motions. Getting productivity out of them will be like trying to coax a cow down some stairs.)

Here's a practice you can apply both with these troubling employees and with any new ones you hire. Invite the lagging employee to your office. Describe the *behaviors* that you see that trouble you. Do not attack the person or the person's character. "You are lazy" isn't going to get you anywhere. Instead, for example, say: "I notice you're always early for work, and that's good. But I also notice that you take about 20 minutes each morning to chat with your team. I'd rather have you come in on time and get right to work." Then ask if the employee can tell you what his job is and what he's supposed to do. You'll be surprised the first few times you do this at how poorly many workers understand what they are doing and why it matters to the company. That's when you pull out a job description—and for the rest of this scenario, follow the script below for new hires.

For a new hire, the very first thing I do is sit down with them and ask them lots of questions unrelated to work. Without getting too personal, I get to know who they are as people, before I try to get to know them as employees. This accomplishes two things: It shows my employees that I care about them as people as well as employees, and it shows them, quite frankly that, although I'm their boss, I'm not a bad guy. I might even know a joke or two!

Typical topics that I like to inquire about are schooling, hometown, children, five-year professional plan, hobbies, favorite music, that kind of thing. I share a little about myself on the same topics, but the focus is on them.

I do this because I'm genuinely interested in them, but I'm also starting to establish trust and build a relationship. I believe that if my employees know just a bit about who I am, they will be more apt to understand my leadership philosophy and feel comfortable asking me questions. The reality is that people who enjoy their work and like who they work for (after all, they applied for the position) are more productive than people who hate their jobs and/or live in paralyzing fear of their employer.

Once the new employee and I spend a few minutes getting to know each other, I get down to the main reason why I invited them to my office. (If you're zoned-out from reading too much or too fast, please take a sip of coffee and focus: This is important.) When employees first start working for you, you *must* tell them what their job is. I know that might seem dumb, but studies and practical applications have shown that a staggering number of employees have never actually been told what to do when they come to work. They know that their position is "warehouse assistant" or something, but they don't actually know what they are expected to do. So they come to work and try not to mess anything up or get in anyone's way.

An employee who knows exactly what she is supposed to do is likely to be motivated and productive. People naturally develop patterns and become more efficient the longer they do something. We become more comfortable with our tasks, we learn things, and we feel good about our output because it has transformed from being a series of tasks to being our job. We feel pleased with the results of our efforts.

In the initial meeting, you can tell your new hire what her job is in any way you wish. If you are partial to spreadsheets, use them. I prefer a simple Word document with a complete job description (over time I've created a series of templates on my computer for every position we have). Also included on the sheet is a list of names and the contact info of people the new hire will be working with frequently, and how they fit into the big picture.

I give her a copy of her job description and encourage her to take notes, telling her to feel free to stop me with any questions she has along the way. We go line by line through the document. I encourage her to make use of our mandatory open-door policy, and tell her it's her responsibility to ask questions whenever she needs answers.

Once that's done, I conclude your meeting with this: "What are your questions?" If she says that she doesn't have any—very well. I just remind her that when one comes up, she knows who to ask, pointing to the sheet.

Once this task is accomplished, you will find that your employees and new hires will be much more productive. That's because they have a connection with you. Thanks to your investment in getting things clear, they know exactly what they are supposed to be doing, where they fit in the grander scheme of your business, and that their efforts will make a difference.

S.G.

Would Someone Please Take My Meeting Out Back and Shoot It?

Consider meeting efficiency as the difference between life and death.

FOR THE MOST PART, I hate meetings, mostly because I don't plan many of the ones I attend. It didn't always used to be this way; it just kind of happened little by little, over time. Early in my career, I thought meetings meant people who were invited into the conference room were really important people—critical to the success of the company. Apparently, that was not the case.

My indoctrination

Early in my career, working for my first big company, I was assigned a desk in a small cubicle. Working from this confined space, my cube-mates and I were known as "box people", in reference to our solitary confinement-like work space. From that vantage point, I watched managers, department heads and outside visitors filing into the super-sized conference room across the aisle, and then closing the door for their Big Meetings.

I had been in that room before, strictly to dope it out. It was a big, fancy space full of large-scale furniture, rock-and-twirl leather chairs, impressive presentation gizmos and fancy snacks.

There were several lengthy meetings in that room every day. "How could there be such a need for so many meetings in one company?" I asked myself. I mean seriously, we only had a couple hundred employees in that office. But it seemed everybody important was taking their turn in those big chairs.

Then one day it happened. I received an invitation (more like a summons) to attend a meeting in the big room. I blocked out part of my day on the calendar and told all the other box people about it. It was like one of us from the wrong side of the tracks was moving out into the expensive neighborhood.

I was riding high that day when I came to work. Although I knew everyone at the meeting, it was still strange walking in. My boss's boss was leading the meeting. He explained that the people present were named to form a team to handle a new project for one of our biggest clients. I remember him saying, as I devoured the last bite of my scone, that the pressure was on us and we needed to perform. He told us to expect lots of meetings. Before I knew it, that meeting was over.

So that was my first experience with a Big Meeting. Apart from the announcement, nothing really happened. Nothing was discussed. This perplexed me. No note-taking, no reminders, no tasks... nothing. I thought that maybe in the next meeting we would get down to business.

The following week, we met again. This time, we got a little deeper insight into the project. However, the meeting leader said that the parameters of the project and our job descriptions would be emailed to us. Two days later, we met to discuss our emails, only to adjourn with no more info or next steps assigned.

My altered perception

After four such meetings, I was fed up with this "getting ready to get ready" approach. Others on the team laughed at me. One of the regulars of the meeting circuit explained that the meetings held in that room never really had any substance—that they were more about show than tell and had little to do with action.

Once my team finally started work on the big project, these damn meetings actually began getting in the way of progress. I began to dread them—and besides, how many scones can a guy eat during a week? My disdain for meetings in general took root.

Apparently, many other companies and organizations take the same approach to meetings as my firm did. I used to laugh at my father when he came home late, complaining about the useless meeting that made him miss dinner again. "What's the big deal?" I would ask. He'd just reply that I wouldn't understand until it happened to me. Years later, I was the one grumbling about the same thing during post-work happy hours with fellow sufferers.

My current, realistic view

I know today that meetings can be vital for the success of a project or to share information and ideas openly. They can motivate people, generate new ideas, be a source of good feedback, and provide a time to bond with colleagues. However, they must be planned and run efficiently. Otherwise, they are an unjustifiable waste of time and money.

Research indicates that the average employee currently spends about 30% of her time in meetings. If they are as disastrous as the meetings I endured in my early years, I wish her luck in getting anything done.

My personal research

Later, in one of my own companies, I called a meeting to actually find out what people hated about meetings. It was the best meeting in the history of the company. I became a hero for initiating it, too! Why? Because it was planned and carried out well.

Everyone in the room knew why were gathered and what was on the agenda. First, we asked participants to describe bad meetings they had attended... even ones within our own company. Every single person was able to contribute! They told stories of receiving no advance agenda or being handed one on the spot, boring monologues, bad joke-telling, horrible food, stupid slide presentations, faulty tech set-ups or thundering air conditioning, ridiculous topics, conversations veering into unrelated directions, people doing email on the sly or arriving late and leaving early, no air or unbearable temperatures, late starts and later endings, no conclusions and next steps, and more. Their stories gave me great material later for some of my training seminars and speaking engagements.

My point

There's a growing awareness of the waste that bad meetings generate. Here are few simple tips that will kill off bad meetings and make the ones that survive a genuinely good use of everyone's time.

- Don't meet. Try avoiding holding a meeting altogether, if possible. If you can accomplish your objective via an email, call or hallway chat, do so.

- Don't attend. Don't accept a meeting invitation that wastes your time. Here are meeting requests I accept: I trust your ability to use my time well; I have seen the objective, agenda and time-frames; attending fits my priorities and goals; the meeting is a ceremony awarding me a huge prize; or you want to buy one of my companies or hire me to consult without negotiating my fee.

- Define clear and concise objectives. This will help the moderator to have specific topics to discuss and can fence out unrelated discussions.

- Announce the agenda in advance. An advance agenda is a tremendous way to allow participants to come better prepared. It is instrumental in keeping everyone on the same page.

- Describe responsibilities for all participants. Explain to invitees why they are being asked to attend and request that they prepare for the meeting accordingly.

- Start and finish on time: Enough said.

When it actually comes time to plan, organize and invite attendees, there are also a few items you will want to address regarding the actual meeting itself:

- Invite only essential attendees. Inviting a bunch of people not relevant to the proceedings just complicates everything. Use a "delegate" principle to name one person from a group who can attend and then update the rest of the group, rather than dragging the whole group into the meeting.

- Focus. Starting and ending on time is vital. Design the meeting to keep moving according to your advance agenda. Cover only the elements on the agenda, unless otherwise dictated by new or unforeseen information.

- Plan for new business. Allow time for follow-up questions, new items of concern, announcements, and so forth. Usually this is best done at the conclusion of the meeting.

- Consider comfort and completeness. Room temperature, room set-up (rows or rounds?), refreshments (scones), media equipment, Internet connection, dress code, scheduled bathroom and email or phone check-in breaks, directions to the meeting facility, meeting room access, presentation materials, and items participants must bring are just some of the elements you will need to address for a productive meeting. Professional preparations set the tone and pace for the session itself.

- Conclude with actions. End your meeting with specific, actionable written points on who does what by when.

- Follow-up appropriately. If people fail to do this, much of the point of the meeting can be lost.

As a leader in your business, you have a lot of power to set or change the way meetings are handled. If you take a second to calculate the fully loaded salaries, facilities costs, food costs, and perhaps travel costs to hold a meeting, and then ask, "Is this meeting really necessary?", you may surprise yourself by how many you can take out back and shoot. For the rest, if you establish the expectation that all meetings are run to the highest level of professionalism, you'll earn back the investment in each gathering.

M.P.

Ideas for Office Gift-Giving

Avoid awkward situations with these helpful tips.

HOLIDAYS AND BIRTHDAYS are occasions that everyone loves—except at work. At work, they can be awkward, obligatory occurrences that nobody likes—neither the givers nor receivers. The potential for emotional discomfort, hurt feelings, and misinterpretation is staggering. If your gift is too expensive, your co-workers will feel uncomfortable about their shabby gifts. If it's lame, in bad taste, or inadvertently hurtful, the recipient will be uncomfortable because he or she will have to fake liking it. And if it turns out you're the only person who didn't give a gift, good luck. We reached out to a number of contacts in an informal survey for this section, and came up with some fresh, helpful ideas. A common theme is that a lot depends on your corporate culture and the number of people involved.

Office Gift Policy. Why not be pro-active and set a company policy that personal gifts (from one person to another) aren't expected? Consider group gifts. Making gift-giving a group event can minimize a lot of awkwardness. And let's face it: if a group agrees that everybody chips in a small amount, you can wind up with a nice gift budget.

A nice middle ground is to have a coffee break, a pizza lunch, or similar treat on special days. For a sizeable company, holding one on the first workday of the month for all the birthday boys and girls keeps the partying in perspective.

If you don't agree with such a policy, and do decide to get someone a gift on your own, make sure it's not too expensive or much better than what you think others are going to get. Buying a lavish gift can make you look like you're trying to improve your situation at work through favoritism or bribery. It's also a good idea to give the gift in private, instead of making a big production out of it in front of the rest of the office.

Regardless of whether you've decided to buy the gift yourself or have agreed to go in as a group to chip in, it's a good idea to set a budget.

What to give? When looking for a gift, thinking hard about the recipient's interests and lifestyle is obviously smart. Popular items include these:

- Coffee shop gift certificate, coffee paraphernalia

- Laptop bag

- Concert tickets

- Coupon for lessons the recipient would love to follow: dance, boxing, gardening, writing…

- Yoga sessions

- Massage or other treatments at a spa, like manicures or pedicures

- Electronic golf scoring system

- Subscription to a favorite magazine

- Donation to a favorite charity

- High-quality pen

- Gourmet gift basket

- Restaurant gift cards

- Hotel gift cards

- Diaper service for new parents

- Gift cards: iTunes, Amazon.com, other e-retailers or local businesses

We discovered mixed feelings about whether or not gift cards were a good or bad gift for a boss. While some thought they were versatile and useful, others thought they were drab and thoughtless. Personally, I would love to get a gift card or gift certificate, because then the chances are good that I could actually get something I really want. Everyone is different, however, so feel things out before making a purchase. If our list still doesn't spark any brilliant ideas, do some clever detective work!

It's usually a good idea to rule out gag gifts that may offend or insult, gifts that may appear to be sexual in nature, and gifts that contain vulgar or inappropriate language. If you are unsure, err on the side of caution. Here are some examples of what we concluded were bad ideas. "Dummies" or "Idiot's Guide" books; sexy lingerie; awkward, profane or offensive T-shirts or similar gifts; food and drink the recipient won't appreciate; bathroom scales; or perhaps non-returnable items.

If, as the leader of your company, you want to give everybody in it gifts, ensure that they are of equal value (we exclude bonuses here because usually they reflect performance and other variable factors). Holiday gift-giving is not a good time to play favorites. A few ideas:

- One-on-one lunch with you (where you pick up the tab)

- Time off (outside of sick days or paid vacation days)

- A token gift on employees' hiring anniversary or on their 5th, 10th, etc. anniversaries

Don't neglect the potential for creative, sentimental gifts or mini-events that are keyed to the recipient or occasion. One employee was leaving full-time work and setting up a home office to work for her company as a freelancer while raising a family. She was astonished to receive the chair from her former office to put in her home office, so she wouldn't forget her friends at work!

Office Relationships and Business: The Do's and Don'ts

All good things are good—until they go bad.

I AM NOT a philosopher, but intimate relationships and business typically mix like a vegan and a veal chop or a hamburger and a heart attack. It's your choice, but I think you'll agree they can be dangerous.

Have you ever found yourself in a relationship with a co-worker, or do you know someone else who has been in one? Many of us have experience with this issue, in one way or another. When you look back on the experience, or you survey the research, it seems clear that inter-office romances are a terrible idea; especially if the relationship did not exist prior to the two people being employed by the same company. Here are some recent findings, including data from Spherion Staffing Services and from consultant Karen E. Klein:

- 36 percent of single respondents would consider dating a co-worker (declining from 42 percent in 2005)

- 57 percent of US companies surveyed have no written policy on the subject

- 22 percent of co-workers who dated eventually married

- Obviously, a relationship between a superior and subordinate is loaded with extra complications

- Romances in smaller companies cause more problems all around

- Even with no written policy, an employer can become involved in legal proceedings when gossip related to a romance is ignored by management

- Gossip, displays of affection, banter that offends others and the couple's work habits can all undermine morale or even become grounds for a hostile atmosphere

It's one thing to be involved with someone who then becomes a co-worker or business contact, but it's a completely different animal altogether when the relationship is built after the two began working together in a company. With that said, I am not saying that a relationship built in the office can't or won't work. But more often than not, they fail, and when they do, it can be ugly and uncomfortable for everyone involved (including everyone else in the office). In short, a professional business environment is no place for personal issues and drama.

Just remember one thing: If the potential for a wonderful relationship exists or could exist, then at the very least, be prepared for the "what if". Let me illustrate the "what if" by asking three simple questions:

1. Are you prepared to have the new potential flame learn intimate details about you that everyone in the office could later hear about?

2. Could you imagine working together if things go South (and I don't mean Tijuana)?

3. If the transition were necessary, would you consider a job change in the event of a nasty breakup?

If you answered "Yes" to all of these questions, then you're probably okay. However, if you answered "No", then you may want to hold off building romantic relationships with members of your office environment or professional community. No matter what, be sure that you have thought about all of the possible consequences and remember that nothing is guaranteed in life or relationships, so be smart about matters of the heart while being clear about who you are and where you want your career to go.

M.O.

Delivering Bad News Quickly

If you have bad news, don't delay or avoid delivering it. Moving forward can even have a positive impact on the outcome.

IT IS NATURAL for you to move quickly when you have is good news to report. The challenge arises when the news is bad.

A business needs to maintain momentum on a number of issues every day. Dealing with bad news quickly will protect your momentum. Drawing out bad news often makes things worse, because the longer it takes for a problem or issue to surface, the less time those affected have to react, formulate a new plan, or solve the problem. If a program needs to be terminated or changed, it is always better to deal with the issue as soon as facts are clear, rather than later. If an employee has a performance issue, it is better to discuss that issue immediately, limit its negative impact to the company, and take corrective action.

Too often, we delay taking action on a negative issue, hoping that circumstances will change or another alternative will be discovered. But the delay distracts us from our business focus, prolongs the corrective process, and often creates a more difficult outcome. It requires discipline and focus to handle things quickly and directly.

Here are some tips on delivering bad news quickly:

- With personnel issues, try to take to acknowledge any strengths or positive potentials that will provide balance to the bad news.

- For business initiatives and policy changes, recap the development of the problem, explain the value of what was learned and any options that were considered but rejected, and then describe the benefit of the action you've chosen.

- Depending on the situation, consider inviting group discussion to address questions, allow emotions to be aired, and explain the importance and value of a tough decision. Then, proceed immediately with the decision.

- If the decision is emotionally difficult for you, focus on the results you hope to achieve. It sometimes helps to tell yourself that this bad news session will be over in two hours, for example, and then you can begin carrying out the decision. There is always a clear benefit in getting it over with and moving forward.

- Be aware that your team will look to you for reassurance and take stock of your demeanor as they react to the bad news. You don't want to deceive them, but if you can present a confident, informed, in-charge air, you can establish a productive atmosphere to begin the response phase.

You may not be able to eliminate the impact or reality associated with bad news. After all, in business, bad news happens to everyone. What puts great businesses ahead of the rest is their ability to react to adversity.

Lame Excuses—A Sign of Trouble?

*Listening and probing, plus problem
solving, can go a long way.*

THERE ARE TIMES WHEN EXCUSES are valid and necessary, often paired with apologies. However, in business, a pattern of frequent excuses may be a sign of a larger problem. Let's assume for the moment that you, as leader and manager of your team, are the one hearing the excuses, not making them. However, if the shoe fits….

Excuses come into play when someone didn't do what was expected, misjudged something, or did something that had negative consequences. They may come from your team or from vendors. Of course, it's always best to be pro-active and alert people affected by a problem before it snowballs. That not only gives everyone a chance to plan around the problem, but it also builds your credibility, even when your performance isn't what was expected. But for now, let's suppose you didn't get a heads up, the problem is now evident, and all you hear is excuses.

You face a couple challenges. Is the excuse a symptom of a contributing problem that needs addressing? Is it a white lie covering up something entirely different (someone is burned out, not suitably equipped or competent to do something, or struggling with issues that interfere with action)?

It's important not to get sucked into a lengthy, dead-end discussion about the excuse itself. Some people really believe that offering an excuse almost solves the problem, when of course it doesn't. They don't seem to be aware that poor or unreliable performance—the situation that makes the excuse necessary—undermines their credibility.

Here are some classic business excuses:

- Weather

- Traffic

- Equipment malfunctions, server down, computer crash

- Miscommunication about expectations or deadlines

- Illness, injury, physical impairments (to the person or a colleague or family member)

- Vacation or personal time off not planned for

- Personal issues

- Someone who owed the person essential things needed to complete the task didn't deliver

- Slammed with other projects

You'll rarely hear someone say,

- "I'm falling in love and can't concentrate", or "I'm having family problems and can't concentrate."

- "I just felt lazy."

- "I hate this job and that task in particular, so I just don't do it."

- "We realize now that we can't do (or deliver) what we promised."

- "I frankly have no idea how to do what's expected and I'm scared I'll get fired when somebody finally figures that out."

- "I'm having a fight with X and don't want her to succeed, so I'm sabotaging her."

You can begin to see why listening past the excuse is very important. Let's look at some ways to chase down what's needed and get to the true causes that triggered the problem.

How to handle no-action or non-delivery problems

- Say, "I notice that X has (or has not) happened. Can you please tell me when it will (or will stop happening)?"

- Or say, "I need to review the project documents you promised to send me yesterday. Can you deliver them today?"

If you get a satisfactory answer (not a fishy excuse), move on to when you can expect what's due to happen. If you smell a fish, probe deeper, not necessarily in a bossy way. For example:

> **You** (not focusing on the non-delivery, rather on what's expected): I haven't seen that report you were going to give me yesterday. Can you get it to me

by 4 this afternoon?

Sally: Well, maybe not. My computer is acting up.

You (problem solving): Can you use Sarah's to complete the report?

Sally: Um, well, maybe. It just takes a long time to do.

You (testing the story): That shouldn't be. Do you know Excel pretty well?

Sally: Uhhh, not really.

You (taking action, not getting bogged down): Okay, let's deal with this in two steps. Let Sarah complete the report. But starting today I want you to spend one hour a day taking the online tutorials. We'll set up a skills test for you at the end of this month. I think you'll like it when you can work faster.

Sometimes entrepreneurs want so badly to succeed that they become blind to the factors that prevent others from performing (as if strength of will could speed up your Internet connection speed). Or they are naïve, or reluctant to admit it when a colleague or vendor isn't performing as needed. They may mistakenly give people too many chances to improve, or hold back valid criticism, rather than neutrally assessing the situation and taking unpleasant but needed actions. When you hear excuses, particularly repeated ones, it's time to dig deeper and address whatever you uncover.

Severing Ties with Lackluster Employees—the Fair Way

Let your poorly performing employees go fairly and efficiently and you'll still be able to sleep at night.

MY LEAST FAVORITE part of being an entrepreneur is having to tell someone to pack up their things and not come back. That they are fired.

Even if she turned out to be the laziest, rudest, most incompetent employee, I feel some guilt because, as their boss, there's always a chance that I failed to warn her, advise her, make her aware of how things needed to be done, describe what she was doing wrong, or point out what she could have done to improve. If you're like me (and I've discovered many business leaders are), you can't help but wonder, as you let someone go, if the poor performance was related to your management. To combat this, I have developed a simple but thorough system to successfully coach lackluster employees without feeling like a jack-in-the-box executioner. I call it the Three-Strike Rule. The name comes out of the game of baseball, where batters have three chances to hit the ball, missing three times before they are out.

Big deal, you say: Just let her mess up three times and then fire her. Sounds easy. That would be easy, but I don't feel good about that approach. It doesn't seem fair to me, because as those three chances slide by, I haven't done anything as a manager. I haven't tried to change anything. I would have trouble sleeping at night if I gave someone the ax without helping them get better, even if I waited to count to three.

Quite frankly, if you hired her, you believed she was likely to be qualified with the skills and performance it takes to be successful at your company. The initial meeting we discussed in a previous section should have launched the employer/employee relationship with clear understandings of responsibilities and expectations. With that, you've given this person many of the tools she needs to be successful.

Still, despite that launch, it doesn't seem like she's getting it. Something isn't quite right about her productivity, efficiency, attitude, etc. This is where the Three-Strike Rule comes into effect.

Strike One: Ground Rules. If someone isn't performing well or has made a significant mistake, the first step should be to ensure that she understands her job description. Don't take her word for it, ask her to tell you. Bring out her job description and review it together. If she asks if she is in trouble, say "no," because she shouldn't be. Strike One should be a fact-finding mission. Determine whether there is a communication disconnect. If you discover that she might not understand her role, take this time to correct her. Encourage her to ask questions or seek clarification; ensure she knows that the only bad question is the one never asked.

It's a good idea to keep notes about the meeting, even if it's just a brief list of discussion points on your copy of the job description. Ask your employee to initial and date it. That underlines the seriousness of the conversation and comes in handy if you need to refer to it later.

If you share a story about another employee who had the same problem or made the same mistake, avoid using names. Even if this employee seems to know exactly what she is *supposed* to be doing, discuss each item on her job description anyway. Wrap up your meeting with two questions:

- What can I do to help you?

- What are your questions?

Typically, you'll get negative answers for both questions. You can feel good about doing everything you could, as a manager, to help her. More often than not, your lackluster employee will realize that she is on your radar now, and address the issues she's been having. But in case Strike One doesn't work and you see more of the same problem, move on to Strike Two.

Strike Two: A Swing…and a Miss. Assuming the first meeting went well and after a bit of time, your employee is back to her lackluster performance, it's now necessary to hold a Strike Two meeting. Remember, as a manager, you are in charge of the situation. Don't lose your temper, no matter how frustrated you may be, as that shows a lack of self-control. Your employees will wonder, "How can he expect us to follow him or rely on his ability to control this company if he can't even control himself?"

Keep it neutral at all times, but stay firm and don't tolerate excuses, because at this phase of the Three-Strike Rule, you could expect to be pitched some doozies. Excuses and legitimate issues are of course two very different things.

Your employees are people, and people sometimes have real issues. If someone can't seem to get to work on time, "I just can't seem to wake up" is an excuse. "My son was just diagnosed with leukemia, his father left us three years ago, and the only doctor's office that will accept my health insurance is on the other side of town" is a legitimate issue.

Don't be closed-minded. Taking the time to help your employees with their legitimate personal issues is what sets great managers apart from good managers. Taking the opportunity to be a good person and a strong leader for your subordinates will instill a sense of loyalty that often pays back dividends in the other direction. If a slightly better job opportunity comes around, studies have shown that employees will sacrifice a minor gain in income in order to stay with a company led by someone they trust and respect. So be aware that you create a tangible value, as a manager, simply by being a good person.

Assuming you don't uncover news that alters the whole situation, at this meeting, the focus should be on the employee's shortcomings. Begin with a review of your notes from the Strike One meeting:

> "On June 4th, you and I discussed your responsibilities. Basically they are X, Y, and Z. I know that you understood your responsibilities at that time because you very clearly described them to me. However, lately, your work has been less than acceptable…."

From there, go on to point to examples of the behavior and performance problems that have occurred since the first discussion and show her how she hasn't been meeting the company's expectations. Re-clarify what you expect from her. This doesn't have to be a replay of the Strike One meeting, but a quick refresher of what her key responsibilities are.

Finally, warn her of termination. Don't beat around the bush about this or try to use a bunch of flowery euphemisms to soften the blow. Remember, this is business. Ensure your employee understands what is at stake.

> "If your performance does not change, you may lose your job here."
> "I want you to know that you are under review for termination."
> "Your performance has put you at risk of termination."

A surprising number of people don't really grasp that *termination* means getting fired or losing their job. Or they are a bit in shock at the moment, and aren't hearing or thinking clearly. If you think this might be the case, probe to make sure your employee fully gets the message. Don't just ask "Do you understand?" but rather, ask, "Do you understand that you may lose your job if we don't see real improvements?"

It is really important that your lackluster employee give you some kind of affirmative answer here. Once she has made it clear that she understands the gravity of the situation, wrap up your meeting with your two key questions:

- What can I do to help you?

- What are your questions?

Once again, you may get a negative reply, or just a penetratingly cold stare at the floor. Although the meeting wasn't pleasant, you can still take comfort in having done about everything you could.

If you like, schedule a follow-up meeting with the employee in a week or two. This will either give you an opportunity to praise your employee on a successful turnaround, or, if the turnaround hasn't been complete but she is noticeably making progress, tell her what she's doing right, and what she could do to continue to improve.

If you haven't seen any improvement, or you see your employee's poor performance continue, your scheduled follow-up could be a good time for Strike Three. As before, it's a good idea to keep notes about your Strike Two and any intervening follow-up meetings, too, initialed and dated by the employee. In case Strike Two doesn't work and your employee still fails to improve, you'll have to move on to Strike Three.

Strike Three: You're out. Again, this shouldn't be a verbal lashing or loud-voice session. If you've been following the steps in the Three Strike Rule, it shouldn't have to be. That's because, due to your first two meetings, your problem employee and you should be on the same page by now. At this point, there shouldn't be any surprises. Although I prefer the Strike One and Strike Two meetings to be one-on-one, I sometimes include an appropriate third party in this meeting.

If your company is pretty sizeable and your lackluster employee has a more immediate supervisor than you, the supervisor can be the third party. Other candidates can be a personnel or office or financial manager (assuming you don't have a human resources department yet). Before the employee arrives, I usually advise this third person not to say anything unprompted, because I like to maintain control of the meeting. I ask the supervisor whether or not he or she wants to add anything at the end. I always remind them to keep it professional and constructive. "That's what you get, jerk!" does not qualify.

Open the meeting with a very brief recap of the first two meetings and note what has happened since the second one. Tell your employee clearly and slowly that you are terminating her. Use your notes from the first two meetings to back up your points and talk about performance, not character. This helps prevent your employee from taking the termination personally, because you are backing up your decision with performance-based facts, figures and examples.

Depending on your employee's reaction, the Strike Three meeting could be as long as the other two, or it could last just as long as it takes for your employee to get up and storm out of your office. Keep in mind that she is allowed to be upset, but do your best to maintain that your place of business is an office, not a circus, and only professional behavior is tolerated. If your employee starts crying, offer tissues; just don't let it affect your decision. At this point, it's too late for second-guessing. If you start back-pedaling, you will appear unprofessional and weak, which can damage your position with everyone in the office.

If you feel yourself start to falter, look down at your notes from the first two meetings and recall how many times you've not only explained your lackluster employee's faults, shortcomings and failures, but also how many times she has said she understands the situation and its seriousness. You wouldn't have gotten to this point if you hadn't already heard these confirmations. Remember, it doesn't mean you don't like her; this is business. It is likely at this point that she will be happier working elsewhere anyway. Whether she apologizes for her behavior or not is irrelevant. You have very clearly and repeatedly set the standard, she has very clearly and repeatedly shown she has understood your terms and accepted your challenge, and she has repeatedly and conclusively fallen short of your organization's and your own expectations.

A situation like this demonstrates why clarity and decisiveness are two skills an entrepreneur needs to lead a company. You are a rock that others trust, depend on, and follow for guidance. Make a decision and stick to it; always be fair, and keep your personal opinions and emotions out of your business decisions. The bottom line here is that it's never fun to let someone go. If it's a performance-based decision, however, as long as you follow the steps listed above, you should rest easy. You'll know that you did everything you possibly could to guide your employee to success, and that unfortunately she was not able to perform as expected, or she perhaps chose to fail.

S.G.

CHAPTER IV
Strategic Thinking and Acting

Diversification vs. Strategic Focus

Diversification is a good thing, right?
Well, not always. Here's why.

WE ALL HAVE HEARD about how diversification—having more than one line of offerings—can spread a business's risks and raise the odds of success. Giant global businesses do this effectively—think of India's Tata Group, which manufactures steel but also makes cars, health care products, and many other diverse goods; or General Electric, which is into practically everything.

But there's a catch. Yours is not a giant global business (yet). So if you are tempted to diversify your offering, be sure you aren't stretching your business too far. It is too easy to get excited about a new thing to deliver, and to end up losing focus on your core business. Don't assume that lots of different things going on in your business means they are all good things. Not exactly—unfocused activity can sink your business.

As an entrepreneur you probably have lots of ideas and not enough time or resources to tackle them all. You find it tempting to branch out, try something new, add a service. But when businesses put their hands in too many cookie jars at one time, they get into trouble. Lots of great ideas get thrown around with equal excitement. But either nothing actually gets to market, or the new offering is marketed inadequately (due to limited budgets and lack of deep experience). And it flops. That in turn drags down overall profits, and the mainline offering can suffer by being neglected in the process. Small businesses can only take action on so much.

It's great to be involved in multiple initiatives at the same time. But before you divert time and resources to something new, ask yourself: Does this fit with our core offerings? Can we realistically hope we'll successfully execute on all fronts without harming our cash cows? As a leader in your business, you have to corral your team and ensure everyone is laser focused on the things that will build and protect success.

There are tons of small businesses that sell too many different things. They clearly don't remember why people patronize their core business. I don't go to the car dealership to buy a shirt, nor do I go to the mall when I'm shopping for a new house. I can't imagine that a car dealership will never see a huge-bottom line impact by selling nostalgic car t-shirts one by one, compared to the hefty hourly fees it can charge for repairs, the 35% markup it can make on replacement parts, and routine preventative service charges that regularly flow in.

Businesses that succeed via diversification usually take on new offerings that are in some way related to their core offering (e.g., the cable company offers not only cable, but telephone and Internet service). Vertical diversification offers essentially the same product in different channels of distribution or sale. Horizontal diversification offers essentially the same product to different types of users. In that car dealership, they have three primary revenue-producers: vehicle sales (new and used), vehicle service, and parts. How can t-shirts possibly fit in? Shirts simply sap the energy and attention of the dealership, contribute little to profit, and the main business will suffer.

How to know when diversification is good

It's amazing how many businesses attempt to compete in industries that are unrelated. If you just can't resist a tempting new opportunity, at least try to focus on something that has some connection with your core products and services. Go back to your business plan and look at what you said about your company's mission and goals. Then ask:

- Does this idea support your core business and mission, or lead away from it?

- Does the new initiative fit with your core offerings in a logical way?

- Will your current customer base find it a good match, a natural enhancement?

- Does your team have the expertise to support the new idea? Learning curves are expensive and risky.

- Can your systems and resources support it? Consider your accounting, storage, sales force, website, marketing efforts, and other important resources.

- Can you objectively say this new thing leverages what you're good at now?

Don't ignore the power of consolidated marketing efforts either. Imagine, the more unrelated verticals a business has, the more marketing lists it will have to buy or create, the more tradeshows and conventions it will need to attend, the more trade journals and magazines it will need to advertise in. It may not be worth all the effort and additional expense for the eventual bump in the bottom line—if there even is one.

Don't spread yourself too thin and don't forget where you came from, what you're good at, and why your customers buy from you. Remember these fundamental things and you and your business should do just fine.

Two Heads Are Better than One:
A Practical Analysis

*In business, 10 percent of something is
always better than 100 percent of nothing.*

OFTEN, MORE THAN ONE individual is responsible for building a wildly successful business or conceptualizing a brilliant business idea. Will one rower in a large rowboat win in a race of large boats filled with teams?

Too many entrepreneurs attempt to do everything themselves. They do this for many reasons. They believe they understand the business's goal best, they don't trust those who don't have a vested interest, they want 100 percent control, or they don't want to share any of the fruits of their labor with others. Although all of these reasons seem to be valid concerns, in fact this thinking is not always realistic.

The reality in most companies is that the even if the owner keeps 100 percent of the profits in a small, one-person operation, those profits could be less than what that person would have made in a properly staffed and well-organized business, even if she only receives a portion of its profits as a partner. By involving others in your business, especially individuals who specialize in different facets of business, you can maximize not only the efficiency of your business but its effectiveness in the marketplace.

Don't be afraid to partner with people who can bring exceptional skill sets and relationships to your business. Below are examples of professionals who can enhance your business's success and keep costs way down.

- Lawyers (business contracts; copyright, patent or trademark filing; intellectual property protection)

- Accountants (tax advantages, bookkeeping, financial planning, getting funding)

- Web designers (websites, social media networking, internet marketing and search engine optimization)

- Engineers (product development, software, manufacturing facility management, workflow systems management)

- Sales professionals (building a sales force, maximizing sales results, streamlining the sales model and moving product for commissions rather than fully-loaded hourly or salary expenses)

Unless you have the perfect business (i.e., it's something everyone needs, there isn't any competition, and your products cost next to nothing to produce and store), you should consider partners, co-founders and investors with active participation and member interest to grow your business to the next level and beyond.

M.O.

How to Evaluate Your Competition

"Know thy self, know thy enemy. A
thousand battles, a thousand victories."

—Sun Tsu

A PROFESSIONAL SPORTS team spends all week preparing for their upcoming game by practicing and training, but also by evaluating their competition's strengths and weaknesses inside and out. Similarly, an entrepreneur shouldn't go into a business without knowing everything about the competition. You've got to know what you're going up against.

The first thing you need to understand is the difference between direct and indirect competition. Direct competition is a company that offers the same products or services to the same niche market as you do. Indirect competition is a company that offers the same product or services as you do, but to a different market than yours. For example, Burger King and McDonalds are direct competitors. In contrast, Pizza Hut, Subway, Taco Bell and KFC are examples of indirect competitors. While they all are fast food chains, they all market different *types* of fast food: pizza, cold-cut sandwiches, tacos, or fried chicken. If you want fried chicken, there isn't much competition, but if you're hungry and could go for anything, then all of a sudden, competition emerges.

Once you've established who your direct competition is, research those companies as much as possible. If your competitors are publicly traded companies, buy a small number of shares in those companies. That way you can receive and study their annual reports, which disclose information on current performance, future plans for expansion into different regions and the release of future products or services. Also, you can see if their sales are increasing or decreasing. You can also get on their email list for newsletters and the like.

If your industry has very little competition, that can be a good and bad thing. The good is obvious—you have very little to compete against. But that could mean that you've unfortunately chosen an industry that is in decline. Maybe the competition bailed out two years ago.

If appropriate, you should also conduct various in-person market research exercises on your competition. For instance, visit your local competitors' stores as a mystery shopper. Look at layout, signage, pricing, promotions, opening hours and so forth. Are there any things here you can do better? Browse around on their website. Is it easy to navigate and place orders? Also, take a look at their ad campaigns and marketing materials. What are their strong and weak points?

Take notes on price-points, atmosphere, quality of product, customer service, and knowledge of their products and services. Also, how busy are the locations? Talk to the employees. Ask them which days are the busiest. Use this information to then outshine your competition. If their customer service is horrible, use that against them and let you future customers know that you'll offer outstanding customer service. If their weak point is a failure to market adequately, a strong marketing campaign can differentiate you from them.

So far, we've only talked about direct competition, but indirect competition is just as important. An indirect competitor, while not in the same industry, is still competing for that dollar. Let's say you're trying to open a miniature golf course; your competition isn't just other miniature golf courses. You also have to consider bowling alleys, ice cream shops, movie theaters, and fast-food chains as your indirect competitors. They're all searching for those families' discretionary entertainment dollars. A lot of families have to make the choice on where and how they would like to be entertained. Your ultimate goal is to have them spend that money with your establishment, rather than the competition down the street.

Often, if you've been in an area a while, you may not have to conduct much research to know what direct and indirect competition is out there. However, if for example you are trying to open a second business location out-of-state or in another country—a place you haven't spent much time—the Internet can be a great place to start. If you want to open a copy center in Melbourne, Australia and your only other copy center is in Tokyo, start by searching the Internet for "copy centers Melbourne Australia". Travel to see them with the same detective agenda as we mentioned above.

Obviously, you'll be way ahead if you do this work before launching your start-up. But even after your business is launched, evaluating your competition regularly is a crucial part in keeping your doors open in today's ever-changing economic climate. Build it into your planning, and sharpen up so you keep your competitive edge.

The Power of Effective Time Management

*American employers lose $760 billion per
year in wages paid for wasted workdays.
You can't afford this loss!*

EFFICIENCY AND PRODUCTIVITY aren't just nice concepts: They are vital to your company's survival, ability to compete, and success. If every person in your company knows how to work efficiently and productively, you have a huge strategic advantage over your competition. The old notion of keeping busy doesn't begin to cut it.

Businesses today don't have time for employees who exhaust themselves by standing waist-deep in busy-work, or who rely on antiquated productivity tools and methods to accomplish their goals. It is crucial to step it up and streamline *the way* each person works, with the emphasis on strategy. Below are a few tips on how to be more efficient and productive. Start by making them your own habits and then model and share them with your team.

Create daily task lists and check the list off as you go. It typically works better if you front-load your workday with all of the items that are the most time-sensitive and have real impact—or are most challenging. Don't get caught in the loop of minutiae, avoiding the critical tasks that need to be done. Quit reloading the printer paper, checking emails, refilling a coffee cup, and most of all, avoid lengthy phone calls and conversations. For example, if you have a question, call the necessary individual and ask it. Then thank the person and move on.

Keep focused. People spend too many minutes every day chit-chatting. That adds up to hours every week, days every month, and weeks every year spent on talk that has little or no impact on advancing your business. As an entrepreneur you can't afford to let your team think like the classic bureaucrat. Why do government service offices run so slowly? Because it doesn't matter how many people the employees assist: All that counts is the number of hours they sit there assisting. There's no incentive to hustle. But there sure is for you.

Use goal sheets. It's smart to organize yourself around short-term and long-term goals. This way, you can work step-by-step toward the completion of long-term tasks over the following weeks, months and years. Think how easy it is to overlook or push back items on a task list. Suddenly you realize you've missed an opportunity or slowed down the evolution of a project. My application of this tool is to hold regular meetings (which could be conference calls) where our team reviews goals and plans next steps. *Regular* is whatever is appropriate: daily, weekly, monthly, quarterly—depending on the term of the tasks or projects involved. If you work from a virtual office and don't get to see your employees or co-workers face-to-face frequently, consider sending regular email reminders or build in a system of regular update reports. You don't need to become a nagging boss; it's just a smart work habit. Your goal is to keep people on task and informed about progress and approaching deadlines.

Don't be afraid to use a planner. The format isn't important—use your computer, smart phone, tablet, or even an old-fashioned lined-paper notebook. The key is to *use* the planner. As an entrepreneur you juggle so many things that without some kind of support tool you'll never be able to keep on top of just the top priorities. So don't handicap yourself by trusting to memory or external prompts. Enhance your abilities, productivity and efficiency. Set an example for the people around you and hold them to high standards of accountability as well.

If any of this seems unnecessarily disciplined, think twice. These days, there is no place for idle walks down memory lane. Everything is different, everything is dynamic, and you need to make the most of efficiency and productivity supports to compete.

Making Tough Decisions

Your decision-making ability is a cornerstone to your reputation as a leader. Here are eight proven tips for making momentous choices.

REGRETTABLY, most companies aren't in business to make friends—they exist to make profits. As an entrepreneur, you must be able to take tough and fair decisions to make sure your company works well. The decisions you make every day on behalf of your business may not always please everyone, and they may be extremely hard to make, but you have to make them—first, because you are the leader, and because they are necessary to grow the business, reach your goals, or just survive.

As you know very well, many start-ups operate on scarce resources, facing stiff competition in an arduous economic environment. Economic crises; catastrophic weather; changes in government policy, new tax rules or regulations; increases in the cost of production; critical product failures; sudden market shifts; bad debt, late payments or the bankruptcy of key customers; or the need to fund business expansion or seize unexpected opportunities are just a few of the external forces that can force tough decisions on you. Internal forces can be just as significant: the loss of talent, data, or the breakdown of key equipment; union activity; interpersonal conflicts; family or health crises; high-impact human errors.

Ideally, the tough and fair decisions you make in business will be reasonable, rational and the best possible ones for the circumstances, given the knowledge you have at hand today. You'll almost never have 100 percent certainty, nor 100 percent of the data you need to back up your choices. You may need to consult with inside personnel and stakeholders as well as external advisors before making these decisions, as they have valuable perspectives on the issues that directly affect your business. Don't play the hero and try to go it alone if others can improve your basis for deciding.

Here are eight best practices that can guide you when you're staring a tough business decision in the face:

1. **Listen to learn.** Listen with an open mind to others' opinions on the potential options and impacts. Seek advice from trusted colleagues, particularly those who have encountered a similar situation, and learn how they maneuvered out. Do not try to reconcile conflicting input now. Take it all in and weigh the value of each view objectively and strategically until you think there are no more options to consider.

2. **Let goals govern.** Ensure that the rationale *as well as* the results of your tough decision will be seen and appreciated in the future. Your decision should be seen in terms of increased productivity, increased profit, financial strength, greater customer satisfaction, increased sales and leads, better working conditions, etc.

3. **Consider morale; factor it in if possible.** Critically analyze the impacts of the decision on relationships inside and outside the business. If time permits, conduct a survey, informal or formal, to gauge how the decision is could affect existing and future business relationships and trust. Take morale into account when you weigh options. But also take care not to become a "pleaser", a leader whose goal is acceptance rather than solid business results based on his decisions.

4. **Include *not* acting among your options.** Sometimes it's wiser to not act. Explore whether there are other alternatives for achieving your business goals *without* taking action: That's a decision too. Tough decisions sometimes cause leaders to be viewed as cold-hearted or unresponsive, and that is not good for morale, especially when not acting proves later to have been a better option. Also, if you truly lack data that could become available within a useful time frame, holding the course might be smart.

5. **Prepare for responses.** Lay out all the potential implications of implementing your decision before taking it finally. Take note of possible challenges like industrial actions, civil suits, demonstrations and strikes, low morale, loss of reputation or customers, and so forth. Prepare counter-actions in advance, including back-up and contingency plans. If it is a decision which is likely to be challenged in court, put all the necessary legal mechanisms in place, e.g., hiring, briefing and consulting your legal advisors. If your action is likely to be resisted by trade unions, consult appropriate experts.

6. **Steady and inspire.** You may struggle with fear, depression, frustration, anger and other negative feelings during this period. In dealing

with others, don't put on a phony act, but on the other hand, take your role as leader to heart and try to steady and inspire others. This is no time to be sentimental, vindictive, furious or harsh. Your team is looking to you to help them be their best.

7. **Limit what-ifs to the time before you decide.** While the what-if drill is important as you test your options, it can be destructive once you've picked out your course. As a leader you need to project confidence in your decision to earn the support of those involved. So long as it is fair and reasonable, do not keep asking yourself "what if", as this will only undermine that support. If you have critically analyzed and identified what you are going to reap from the tough decision in the future, go on and implement it. Good business leaders are known for their words and actions, not their doubts.

8. **Tell it like it is.** Make the goal of your decision clearly known to those involved and if possible, to those it may affect. The way you state your outcome can influence your actions significantly. Inform people why the decision has to be made, what it is meant to achieve, and if necessary, why other solutions are less effective. If you have to resist a salary increase request from an employee whose performance is not commensurate with their demand, for example, you might say this: "I appreciate that your cost of living is rising, as is our cost of running the business. As you know, our revenue is down. To keep our doors open we have determined that we have very little room for raises this year. Our goal is to reward our very top performers first and then see about cost-of-living increases if there's money left over. Unfortunately, you are not *yet* one of our top performers. I will let you know if we can give you a cost of living increase in one month, but I would not count on it coming through, based on what I see today."

Let your values and goals as well as your critical thinking skills and business sense guide your strategic thinking when making a tough business decision. Some say that it's in these terribly challenging moments that your very best qualities emerge. If you can view tough decisions as the gateways to new days to play, and work at maintaining optimism and balance, you should do fine. Set the example, steer the course and roll on.

Fire Up the *Right* Passion for Your Business

Passion can be the beauty that entices you to launch the perfect business, or the beast that talks you into a terrible decision.

HOW MANY TIMES have you read or heard the word *passion* in business talk lately? There's "finding your passion" or being "passionate about your work", and a raft of other passionate talk. Although these discussions are clearly sincere and, ummm… passionate, there's one small problem with them. The common way *passion* is used in business talk is somewhat backward. Let me explain.

Think about it for a moment. People typically never get passionate about a sport until a series of events take place. First, they see the new sport. Then, through contagious emotion or excitement generated by others (a wild crowd, the announcers, etc.), they join in, cheering with the others. Have you ever been to a bar when a game on television suddenly captivates everyone there? Before you know it, you're all cheering for the Zimbabwean women's curling team, the Jamaican bobsled team, or Eddie "The Eagle" Edwards—in this case, because they are the underdogs!

I remember finding my way into a popular pub in London a couple of years ago. The people in the joint were glued to several TVs around the place. There was a football game on, but it wasn't the kind of football I was accustomed to watching in the States. Where I come from, it's known as soccer. But there I was, watching the game among passionate fans who were losing their minds as the home team tried to score the go-ahead goal. Hell, I wasn't sure about the rules, but it didn't matter. I was overcome with excitement and passion—and you should have seen me cheering and shouting in that pub. In this instance, passion wasn't the cause of the excitement—it was the effect. You could say *passion infects* people in these situations, like a common cold.

Ask any writer how he or she gets inspired. If they were to wait for passion to come their way before starting to write, the book might never be finished (or even started). For them, once they commit to writing, inspiration follows on its own. The result: *passion develops.*

So how does this relate to business? As an entrepreneur, I would never embark on a new initiative based solely on contagious passion. It might help me identify something I could develop a long-term, committed passion for, enough to study and evaluate carefully before plunging in. After my due diligence, and after engaging with countless people who are involved in and passionate about the business or industry, I can then make an educated decision to move forward with the project. In short, using contagious passion to identify an opportunity and to fuel your creative juices is good; but then stepping back to check it out dispassionately is best before committing.

Think about multi-level marketing (MLM), also known as network marketing, or when viewed negatively, pyramid marketing. Most of these organizations build their industries with contagious passion as the cornerstone—enticing others with huge income potential, free cars and trips, and the vision of a "work-when-you-want" lifestyle. I know this because I have been involved with them myself.

Through their perfectly calculated system of conventions and pep rallies, a spectator or potential enrollee can usually listen to a roster of above-average public speakers who take the stage to tell their stories of success, making the most of booming sound systems and high-tech video production to get the audience fired up about the business and eventually to sign up as distributors.

This concept works! For the franchiser, at least. Some starry-eyed dreamers just fall for the glittery show. However, after returning home to reality, with their contagious passion wearing away (until the next big meeting), the truly successful participants will always tell you that "the multi-level marketing product must ultimately work and also be affordable" if they are going to stick with it and make money. The success stories are about the entrepreneurs who do their due diligence first, then turn the contagious passion (their own or others') into committed passion to drive home sales and sign-ups.

Committed passion carries you forward long-term

When you consider a start-up or a new direction for your company, distinguish between contagious and committed passion. If passion develops and survives, it must be for a reason. Make sure you dig deep first to find out why it's there in the first place. Then, if you like what your investigation has uncovered, it may be time to go for it. Afterward, if you have made that vital commitment and are working toward success, your committed passion will develop and strengthen over time.

M.P.

Three Economic Concepts You Must Master

The first step toward success is getting a firm grasp on the basics.

IF YOU'VE EVER taken a basic economics class, you probably remember a few key terms that dictate the success of businesses in the marketplace. Three concepts are especially important for entrepreneurs to understand: *comparative advantage, opportunity cost,* and *true cost of production.* Learn these and you'll be on your way to speaking fluent Economist.

- **Comparative advantage**. Make sure that you are spending time or money on the things that are your specialty and are an efficient use of your time. For example, don't make your own wiring for an electromechanical product if you can find a source elsewhere, such as a factory in Wuxi, China, to manufacture that same component for a lot less money. When a vendor can provide a product or service more efficiently and/or for less cost than the others in the industry, they have a *comparative advantage* over others. This explains why the world buys coffee from South America, toys from China, lumber from Canada, and customer service from India.

- **Opportunity cost.** Remember, in an earlier section, when we mentioned efficient use of your time? This ties directly into the idea of opportunity cost. Opportunity cost is the item, task or alternative that you are forfeiting by choosing to spend your time or money elsewhere. An example would be if you spend three hours in a machine shop making a widget, then the opportunity cost is what you could have gotten done during those three hours if you hadn't made the widget.

Got it? Good. The tip here is to make sure that you are making the best use of your time by understanding what things you are efficient in doing and what you should outsource to another professional or business.

- **True cost of production.** This is probably the most shocking concept. *True cost* refers to all cost elements related to the product or service development process, from start to finish. The fully-loaded expenses associated with product production or service-providing include research and development, beta testing, sampling, market testing, creating sales material, promoting the product, selling expenses, carrying costs, returns and loss, administrative expenses and other miscellaneous costs associated with that particular product. All of these expenses are real and need to be accounted for and recovered throughout the product or service life-cycle.

Concepts in practice

The above concepts may seem like common sense, but you would be surprised how many small business owners lose sight of the fact that if a business produces a few products or provides a few services, then all of the expenses of the company have to be built into their cost to create a *true cost*. The person answering phones, the janitorial services, the trash service and the utilities, to list a few, all need to be covered. It may seem tedious, but in a successful business with organized financials, all of these line-items are accounted for and built into the costing of the company's deliverables.

Keep this critical survival accounting fact in mind: If you are looking at an expense of the company, then account for it and decide where the money will come from to pay for it. I've seen businesses royally screw up this practice. One unfortunate example is a lawn care business in my area. Their experience shows how ignoring seemingly tiny cost items can ruin a very simple, successful small business.

Before they went out of business, this lawn care company cut my grass once a week for $100 a month. Those 52 cuts yielded them $1,200 a year. If you do the simple math, you'll see that I was paying $23.07 per cut.

Now understand that it took three guys approximately thirty minutes to do my yard professionally. Assuming that the guys were each making $10 per hour, the labor cost for my yard was $15 dollars. Now add up the other costs: for the lawn care equipment, the truck, the trailer, the depreciation associated with all of that equipment, the gasoline and oil to fuel the mowers, the fuel to drive the whole outfit to and from my yard, and the hourly rate being paid to the crew members as they drove over, worked, and drove back.

I'm not going to line item all of this here, but I am positive that it cost the business owner more than the $23.07 I was paying to provide his service, each week. Therefore, it didn't take long for the business to fail. Still to this day, the owner believes that the failure was due to external forces (e.g., rising gas prices, increasing labor rates, competition, etc.).

These economic facts are all real issues that businesses face, regardless of the industry. If you take the concepts of comparative advantage, opportunity cost, and true cost of product into account, you should have a firm foundation for planning and can minimize nasty financial surprises.

Outsourcing Your Projects:
A Moderate View

If someone wants to do something for you, better
than you can do it yourself, for the same cost,
why not let them? And what if it costs less?

IT HAS BEEN impossible to ignore the ongoing controversy about the outsourcing of jobs, often but not always from developed countries to developing countries. Worries about unemployment rates, sweatshops, child labor, the rich getting richer, the poor getting poorer, the vanishing middle-class, the blue collar worker, and an array of other serious issues have swept around the world. Nevertheless, outsourcing is flourishing. It is discouraging that the topic has become so emotionally charged.

Outsourcing has a rainbow of emotion-charged colors associated with it. On the positive side, all the temporary or interim worker services like Adecco, Randstadt, and Robert Half save companies enormous sums. Rent-Execs step into businesses just like a temp receptionist and work there until permanent executives and managers can be found, or until the business is turned around or sold. When you think of it, any time a company farms out work to freelancers, hires an independent sales force, retains an attorney—even when it ships goods—it's all outsourcing, because none of those tasks are being done inside the company by employees.

We just can't do everything ourselves, and we never have. True, exporting jobs across continents and oceans costs local workers jobs every day. But it's silly to view things in extreme black and white terms, on this issue as on most. While we are all entitled to our own opinions, I humbly ask: if outsourcing is economically evil, why is it working? The nice thing about a free market is that it's self-corrective—if an idea is truly bad, it will fail, and vice versa.

A: What do you call it when you take your car to a mechanic and ask him to change the oil for you?

B: Taking the car to the garage.

A: Yes, but it's also outsourcing.

B: No it's not! Outsourcing is bad! I have the mechanic change my oil because he's equipped to do it, he's better at it than I am, and it frees me up to do stuff I'm better at.

A: Precisely. Thank you for that textbook definition of outsourcing, and for the demonstration that outsourcing occurs in all kinds of situations.

One of the proven ways of effectively managing a business is by outsourcing appropriate steps or projects. Perhaps especially in the early days of a one-person start-up, and particularly if you currently work full time at another job, you'll be likely to outsource some tasks. Outsourcing can improve productivity whether you are on your own or you run a business.

By not outsourcing appropriate work, you can miss out on time- and cost-saving opportunities. You may also be incurring opportunity costs, spending more time doing something that you could have someone else do while you concentrate on doing something that perhaps only you can do. For example, if you are currently working full time, you may decide to start a website that will earn you money on the side. If you do not outsource the hosting of this website, you will end up with poorer results, since your website work will eat into your evenings and you will not be able to make any sales while busy with it.

New outsource tools

Traditionally, if you wanted to farm out some work, you would ask around, identify some candidates, check them out, discuss the project, and if all went well, sign them up. That still works. But there are more comprehensive ways to do this, online.

The first step is to find some websites online (like craigslist.org) that can help you recruit people. After selecting a website that is best suited to your needs, you may have to open an account. This account will enable you to post the details of your business or your project on the website. Clearly describe the tasks you expect the outsourcing people to perform for you and also go into details about the project or the business itself. Being explicit at this stage is important for finding a perfect match for your needs.

While you are creating a portfolio on the project or the business that you want to outsource, be clear on the dates that you expect the work to be done. State both the start and end dates, so that you don't experience any delays when you finally outsource the work. Also, ensure that you are realistic when you are setting the dates, as you cannot expect work that will take three months to be completed in two weeks' time. You should then expect to get hits on your account. These hits are made by bidders for the outsourcing jobs.

All bidders have the potential of winning the work, but you will have to be vigilant when selecting a final bidder. This is to ensure that you outsource the work to someone who will actually deliver and not cause you headaches or worse. To do this, ensure that you critically evaluate every bidder's portfolio and also fact-check all the details that they provide. Keep in mind that selecting the cheapest bidder may not render the best results.

S.G.

Eight Ways to Cut Business Travel Costs

Ensure your employees care as much about this as you do. They probably don't know that their jobs depend on it.

TOO OFTEN, employees think that the company they work for is a bottomless pit of money. They care little about their spending while traveling for business and consider it their "right" to live well while travelling on the corporate dime. While you can try to explain to them that your corporate money pit *has* a bottom, you might have more success by also explaining that their pay checks come out of the same pit as their travel budget.

Help them understand by setting corporate travel guidelines. It's pretty obvious that, given the choice between cutting travel costs and corporate downsizing, your employees will be enthusiastic about making choices on the road to help control and cut travel costs. Below are a few examples of ways to cut costs for your road warriors.

1. Car rental

- See if your business can sign up for a frequent-rental program to take advantage of free rental days or rental discounts.

- Instead of renting cars from the well-known companies, seek out the smaller companies that operate outside the airport or travel center (many of these companies may even provide a courtesy shuttle to the airport). Online services can scour listings for really deep discounts.

- Consider renting used cars. These may not be suitable for making calls on customers who might think you're about to go belly up, but for getting from A to B they can be real budget stretchers. Watch out for smokers' cars if that matters to the driver.

- Stay away from the "extras", such as rental insurance, EZ Pass transmitters, GPS systems, and an advance fill-up of gas.

- Pay attention to the fine print for restrictions, such as mileage caps.

2. Food

- If you will be staying in a particular area for more than two nights, look into hotels that offer extended-stay rooms. These rooms come equipped with a full kitchenette. You could head for the local grocery store and put together your own meal at a fraction of the cost of restaurants and hotel breakfasts.

- Take advantage of the free continental breakfasts offered at many hotels.

- Stay away from using the hotel's room service in order to avoid paying unnecessary room service fees as well as exorbitant food and beverage prices. Many companies require their travelers to pay for these charges personally.

- Where possible, bring along your own snacks to help quell hunger cravings.

3. Air travel

- Save money on airline tickets by booking trips a month in advance. Where possible, schedule flights for Tuesday through Thursday and try to fly into alternative airports. For domestic flights, look into discount airlines.

- The Internet is a powerful tool in helping small businesses locate low-cost airfares. To make your searches more efficient, use Expedia.com, Hotwire.com, Travelocity.com and Kayak.com. These sites sift through airfares, hotel rates, and other travel products from over 140 different sources. Choose the offer you want and they will direct you to a site where you can buy the ticket.

- If you will be bringing a lot of luggage with you, then be sure to check the luggage policies and fees beforehand and shop around. When possible, consider shipping materials and samples by a ground service, well ahead of your meeting, or emailing files that your contact can print onsite prior to your appointment (if that's acceptable). In general, try to avoid checking luggage.

- If you will be driving your car to the airport, be sure to park it in a long-term, off-site parking lot to avoid an outrageous expense when you return.

4. Centralize travel planning

Even if your company is small, try not to let employees make their own travel arrangements whenever they feel like it. First of all, that's not their job, and the opportunity cost of their surfing time is directly reducing time for their key role. Also, it is easier to keep track of your travel spending when all the arrangements are made in one place. To save time and money, choose an agency that specializes in business travel and then let them do the research for you. It is simply more efficient to let a travel agent find the best flight or hotel room for your trip, and chances are, they will be more aware of ways you can save. Keep in mind that while travel agencies don't always book the discount airlines, they sure can get you a good price when it's tricky. Also, while frequent flier miles are great (and taxable), staying loyal can prevent you from saving on the discount flights.

5. Create a travel policy

A travel policy is an important document that will help you clarify expectations of employees. When employees have a policy in hand, it eliminates questions about what is and isn't allowed before they leave town. Make sure to be explicit about what is reimbursable and what isn't. Once you have your policy, consistently apply it, including charging back unacceptable items or too-high totals on a meal. And to help cash flow, let employees know that their expense reports are due no later than the end of the month in which the charges were made. Or else!

6. Establish spending limits

When people eat out on their own tab, they are usually able to control their appetites. Make sure your employees exercise that same kind of restraint when they are traveling on the company tab. You can establish daily spending limits for food, cars, and hotel rooms. Or, you may want to be more specific and state an upper limit for each sort of item, including tax and tip. Make sure that these spending limits are clearly listed in your travel policy and on a uniform expense report form.

7. Join your airline's frequent flyer program

If your business travel routinely includes flying, make sure that your company receives the mileage credit and ensuing benefits. Some airline programs even allow the company and the employee to simultaneously earn mileage points. In addition to earning free trips, some airlines also offer business travelers access to their airport clubs, hotel discounts, and other perks, which can help your company save even more. But there's a flip side to this: Be prepared to be flexible and fly discount fare airlines when they present a really better price.

8. Use a corporate credit card

Keeping all travel expenses on one credit card account simplifies book-keeping and eliminates the headaches associated with employee reimbursement checks. For an added bonus, find a card that rewards you with frequent flyer miles, hotel discounts, or other travel perks.

Setting Goals for Long-Term Success

In business, as they say, when you
fail to plan, you are planning to fail.

ALL BUSINESSES, whether small or large, need to define long-term goals so that both leaders and employees have a clear vision of what they are working toward. If you have a business now, or you're thinking about starting one, recognize that financial goals are essential for your success. If you know your goals, read on and see how they measure up. If you are pre-goal, or operating without any clearly stated ones, adapt what follows to your current position. Here are important factors to consider.

The first thing to do is to establish your business's current financial status. In a small or young operation, you may not have top-notch financial reports, or your historical data could be scattered all over the office (or missing, or maybe it never actually existed). It will pay off hugely if you take the time and trouble now to get your basic financial facts organized and accessible. How can you look forward when you don't have a clue where "right here, right now" really is? Get things pulled together, perhaps with the help of outside bookkeeping or accounting help, so you have an accurate balance sheet and profit and loss (P&L) sheet to base further thinking on.

Once that's done, you will already see a bunch of short-term goals emerging. Maybe your clean-up phase revealed that you actually owe more money than you thought. Or made more profit than you thought. Or that very good or very bad cash flow times are just around the corner. So start by listing monthly goals. They will naturally spill over to quarterly goals, followed by annual ones. Before you know it, you will have identified some of your business's long-term goals. Building the goals up by looking further and further ahead in stages enables you to clearly align your operational goals with your financial goals so that you can have fully synchronized goals for your business. Also, by keeping your finances front and center, you won't overextend yourself financially.

Try to create financial goals in relation to the financial performance of the company in its last business year. For example, if it cost you $10,000 to run the business last year, set a goal that in the current financial year, it will cost you perhaps $7,000. Then, if the business made $20,000 in profit in the last financial year, set a goal for, let's say, $25,000 for the current year. The main aim is to set goals that will decrease your expenditure while increasing your income and thus, your business will be profitable. Streamline your staff and increase your work hours if it will mean attaining the long-term goals for your business. Failure to do this may interfere with the progress of reaching your goals.

So far, you probably will have identified goals dictated by today's picture. Now turn on your intuitive, creative, associative powers. Where do you want to be next year, and five years from now? If you don't include goals for moving in those directions now, you may end up stable but not lively and expanding. Identify these goals and map out what needs to happen monthly, quarterly, etc. financially and otherwise to move you where you want to go. Then step back and see whether together, your financial-based and your dream-based goals are viable. Make adjustments until you are confident they are, at least for today.

To keep on track and flag problems as you go forward, establish milestones and measures now that you can use to gauge progress and success. Some logical options are on-time delivery of new products, sales figures, budget and profit measures, and so forth. Some companies prefer to use their monthly or even yearly net income as one measure, while others concentrate on the costs of running the business. Your choice of tools depends on what you want to achieve, so think smart about what you pick. Then figure out how you want to see measurements reported, shared, and acted upon.

Final thoughts: When you are setting long-term goals for your business, don't overreach. If you are not pragmatic, even perhaps conservative, then chances are good that you will not achieve them, or you might die trying. Who loves failure? Not to mention losing face and money if your pie-in-the-sky planning takes your business under, opposite the direction you intended. As they say, growing a business is like running a marathon, not a sprint.

SWOT Analysis: It's Not What You Think

It's about examining your business
honestly and planning for the future.
Discover your own possibilities.

WITH ALL THE CHALLENGES that businesses face, it's nice when a process is invented to analyze the business's many facets, both internal and external, positive and negative, past and future. The SWOT Analysis examines a business's Strengths, Weaknesses, Opportunities and Threats in order to allow leaders to make good decisions and wise adjustments, moving forward. (Note that strengths and weaknesses are analyses of internal factors, and that opportunities and threats are analyses of external factors.)

Too often, entrepreneurs suffer from a kind of internally oriented, forward-focused tunnel vision. They fail to analyze what they've already completed or see what is going on in their industry or in the world around them. Given how rapidly the world is advancing technologically and politically, to ignore the outside world can be financial suicide. It's like the guy who tried to start an oil lamp company the day after Edison invented the light bulb. He failed to read about Edison's breakthrough in the newspaper.

So to broaden and enrich your company's current state and future prospects, try making your own SWOT Analysis.

Strengths: What are you doing well? What resources or intangible assets do you have access to? This analysis is for your benefit, so neither overinflate nor or sell yourself short.

Weaknesses: What does your company struggle with or can it improve upon? If possible, what should you steer clear of? The most common struggles include price points, employee management, continual improvement, and gaps in your methodology or processes. Do any of these apply to you? Again, you're looking at yourself for improvement, so honesty and accuracy are important.

Opportunities: What opportunities can you name that might help your business in some way? Think political changes, favorable tax adjustments or breaks, new grants, a major competitor going under or temporarily cutting back, good press, a new potential investor, etc. Keeping a watchful and creative eye out for opportunities lets you act on opportunities before the competition.

Threats: Threats can come from any direction. The most common is from your competitors. Even if you are on a friendly basis with them, their success can still be a major threat to your business. There are only so many customers looking to buy your product or service, and if the competition is getting most of them, you're not.

Another common threat can come from regulation and taxation. Many entrepreneurs feel these factors stand in the path of a free-flowing free market. While governments admittedly offer benefits, especially in the big picture, even a loosened tax is still a tax, and that's money that can't be reinvested, paid out to employees, or used to expand.

Don't focus only on the governments affecting your local business when you consider threats. Actions by a government halfway around the world can raise the price of your key components, apply sanctions against your products coming into their territory, or cost you a fortune in duties and customs clearance or testing fees. And the fate of distant economies can send ripples that rock your boat completely unexpectedly.

Once you identify threats, try to assess each one by asking exactly how threatening they are, and what you can do to alleviate the threat(s). Adapt and overcome!

The truly wonderful thing about the SWOT Analysis is that the size of your business doesn't matter. It can be used by a giant international conglomerate, an independently owned and operated hot dog stand, and everyone in between. For instance:

Strengths: My hot dogs taste good. People love them!
Weaknesses: I don't have a very tasty bratwurst recipe.
Opportunities: The bank just started advertising business loans for hot dog stands.
Threats: Fred from two blocks over has very delicious hot dogs, too, and also sells bratwursts.

When you try it, remember that SWOT Analysis isn't a problem-solving tool. It is a *problem identifying* tool. We can all agree that identifying a problem is the first step to solving it. The same works with opportunities--the first to discover and respond correctly wins the prize!

On the Look-Out for Opportunities and Threats

Monitoring your environment should be a constant state of mind for an entrepreneur.

AS AN ENTREPRENEUR, YOU MUST constantly be on the look-out for opportunities and threats affecting your business in order to handle them effectively. As we've just seen, it pays to think systematically and to run a continual scan of your business environment. That way you lessen the chance of sudden, full-blown bad surprises, and you can jump on opportunities at the earliest possible moment.

You can identify the opportunities and threats affecting your business by monitoring and analyzing the *internal* and *external drivers* that shape your business's environment. If you set up a grid like the one on page 120, you can begin to fill in the boxes as news comes your way, so you don't lose track of developing situations.

If your company is bigger than a solo enterprise, do this with your team. If you have lots of people, appoint a Look-Out Team and charge them with making a brief quarterly report on developing stories. This can be done live or via email, but the point is to do it continuously and to consider what actions are called for as a result.

In this sample grid, we've sketched in the kinds of comments you or your look-out team could make (obviously, some are contradictory here; they are just illustrations to start you thinking).

This need not be an elaborate document: Think of it as a rolling scoreboard keeping track of the game you're in right now. If it grows to be fairly large, you may want to add a priority column so hot topics get appropriate attention and action. By their nature, topics can appear and fall off the grid as situations or your

Look-Out Team Report			
OPPORTUNITIES			
	Nature of Opportunity	**Sources of Information**	**Possible Actions**
Internal	Talent surplus	Performance reviews	Expand operations with surplus talent
	Resources or cash surplus	Accounting reports	Expand size, markets, production
	Capacity surplus	Production reports	Make more, add new lines using same equipment and people
	New ideas	Customer feedback	New products, services, locations
External	Economic	*Wall Street Journal* article	Increase productivity, improve service, expand
	Cornered Market	Market Test	Grow quickly before competition arrives
	Technological	Vendor tip	Increase production speed, quantity, quality
	Diminished Competition	Market Test	Identify why the competition failed and take action
THREATS			
	Nature of Threat	**Sources of Information**	**Possible Actions**
Internal	Low funding	Accounts	Get a loan or grant, moonlight.
	Talent deficit	Personal talk	Hire more, train existing
	Low morale, motivation	Demand for union meeting	Talk to people, listen more
External	Government	Notification or research	Abide by business and tax laws, make changes
	Competitors	Trade journal, rumor at conference	Improve business quality, add incentives, adjust business model

knowledge about them evolve. Therefore it may be smart to archive each report so you can review old ones conveniently and pick up on discarded items if they become timely again.

Note that the look-out team does have to indicate some possible actions for each opportunity or threat on the grid. This will get team members accustomed to owning a part of the processes of internal change or of response to external events that may become necessary, given what they discover. They in effect can become advocates of sometimes painful adjustments. But on the plus side, they can also be champions for jumping on new opportunities and share in the glory of successes.

This exercise has a way of really engaging people in a company's current and future life. It vividly demonstrates that your company is practically a living organism, and it can become a unifying and motivating focus for your team's engagement in their work as they take ownership of a part of their collective future.

Succession and Disaster Recovery Planning

*Not a barrel of laughs, but good for peace
of mind and protecting your business.*

YOU MAY BE TEMPTED to turn the page and not read this section. After all, who gets a kick out of Doomsday thinking? But read on and think about what could happen if you do nothing to address these issues.

It's surprising how many start-ups and small businesses lack plans for succession in their leadership or for recovering from disasters. It's understandable, on some level, that entrepreneurs are more inclined to focus on the immediate challenges that confront them every day, or on the future. But *particularly* for a fairly new or small business, the consequences of not thinking through and planning for what you can foresee happening can be enormous—and deadly.

Succession planning

Planning for succession—the smooth transition of responsibilities in the event the person currently holding them cannot fulfill them, for whatever reason—need not be a depressing exercise. Take a look at your company's set-up today and ask yourself how you could cover the various functions that make it run, in the event today's incumbents can't perform.

We've all heard stories of the spouse whose mate dies in a plane crash and suddenly has to figure out how the family business works. But even less dire situations can put you out of commission for a while (the slip of a steak knife can take a graphic designer out for a month!). So whether yours is a one-person or many-person business, give some thought to documenting processes, recording where key data is located (physically or virtually), and listing securely your key business contacts and financial essentials (bank, investor, and similar information). Then pick a trusted person to share this information with and store it safely. In the event you can't work for a while, this person can step in or guide another person toward either keeping things running or winding things down.

Suppose now that you have employees who play various roles in your business. If one of them falls sick or abruptly leaves for greener pastures, what happens? Give some thought and open discussion to the idea of cross-training. Try to link up people who naturally interact and ask them to show the other party how their area works, in some depth. Get the warehouse and production people, the admin and finance, and other natural pairings buddied up. They will perform better day to day because they understand the other area's issues and set-up, and in the event that someone needs to step in to fill a gap due to illness or resignation, they can help ensure continuity while you figure out what to do next.

Shining up your stars

A different aspect of succession planning is a lot sunnier. In addition to cross-training, it's good to step back from time to time and ask yourself where the career paths of your people are heading. Do you have candidates who can succeed you in the future, either in your business or outside it? Have you spotted especially talented people who could be groomed to take on higher or broader responsibilities over time? Do people have a feeling they can advance by sticking with you, or are they in the dark?

You can share your thoughts about this, or not; you can share only part or all of your thinking. It's a great incentive for an employee to hear she has a chance to earn a promotion or to step into a more challenging and rewarding role if she prepares for it and demonstrates her ability to deliver. And a longer-term perspective of the possibilities for advancement often wins greater employee engagement and job loyalty today. Make it a regular part of your performance reviews to ask employees where *they* want to go and what they need to get there. You'll often uncover surprising aspects of their ambitions, interests and dreams, which may help you harness their passion and link their success to yours.

Don't skimp on providing your future stars with the tools and learning they'll need along the way. Sure, these things can cost quite a bit, but they are every bit as important as your investments in the latest software or fork lift you just bought. Don't make the classic mistake of making your top salesperson the sales manager without making sure that person has a grasp of sales management, perhaps a coach or mentor, and plenty of supportive feedback as he assumes the role. If you neglect this, you risk losing your best seller from the front line and sabotaging all the other sellers by giving them a terrible boss!

A final thought: consider buying life insurance for yourself as leader, and for key players, naming the company as its beneficiary. Then, in the event of a death, you have some revenue to cover a transition period. Also, ask yourself whether your top team should drive or fly together as a normal practice. You probably will find that your insurer will have guidelines or requirements in these areas, but simple common sense will also tell you when not to take unnecessary risks.

Disaster recovery planning

They say in disaster recovery planning circles that you should protect yourself up to the level that you don't mind losing what is unprotected. In other words, if you can afford to lose a week's work, then weekly computer server back-ups are okay. But in these times, that's a ton of work. A daily back-up with a copy stored off-site is much more reasonable for relatively simple businesses. A duplicate system in another location could be necessary for more complex or highly technical operations.

If you own copyrights or engage in giving advice (even in the form of a user's manual for some gadget) you may need to buy liability insurance or other policies to defend your intellectual property rights. A trusted corporate insurance broker can educate you on these issues.

Data is one thing, but your other assets need protection too. Smoke and motion detectors, sprinkler systems, alarms, and a raft of other things may stretch your budget, but consider the alternative if you don't have them installed and something goes wrong. The same is true for worker safety and insurance against injuries or "acts of God."

We had a very small fire on the upper floor of our building which was quickly extinguished by the sprinkler system – which was the good news. The bad news was that the water then flowed down the side walls of the building, collected on the false ceiling of the floor below, and that ceiling collapsed, spilling water and ceiling tiles all over the call center's computers and phones. A fire no bigger than a cozy campfire halted the business for a couple weeks and cost half a million US dollars to recover from. Thankfully, we had "interruption of business" insurance and we lost no more than personal items in people's work space, for which they were reimbursed as best we could.

Don't neglect low-tech protections as well. It's simple to set up phone chains, in which each person knows whom to call (and has the right phone number) to pass along urgent information (like snow days, or other high-impact events or info). Designate gathering places outside your business and make sure everybody can exit and gather there to be counted safe and sound. Post fire exit maps and signs, and conduct fire drills (including closing fireproof doors) periodically. The fact that your business is small doesn't prevent it from encountering nasty situations, unfortunately.

All these things probably seem like real sidetracks when you're busy with your core business. But think of it as good stewardship that will enhance your odds of living to play another day. You'll never know how many things you avoided or prevented from happening, but you may gain a little peace of mind from proactively addressing them as you build your company's future.

Exit Strategies and Why They Matter

Why think about the end when you're just beginning?

IT'S HUMAN NATURE to relish the novelty and the clean-slate effect that permeates a brand new start-up. With no past, and a clear playing field stretching into the future, it's really a pleasant period. It's a bit like playing house: You'll never be so free to make things up.

That's fine, and the high you may feel in these early days helps inspire and propel you forward, even partly rewarding you for the really long days and nights of work, the worry, and the flat-out ignorance of things you should have known as your business takes root. But even now, you should give thought to the negative what-ifs, in case your business just doesn't work out. How will you wind it up and protect yourself as much as possible if things go south? What level of performance will tell you it's time to stop? It's said that the absence of exit strategies is a major problem for new businesses. It can't hurt to think through some scenarios and have them in the back of your mind in case they ever become necessary.

Perhaps your business is looking pretty healthy these days. It's still smart to kook as far into the future as you can. Where do you want this thriving company to end up eventually? And what role will you be playing as you bow out? If your company continues to survive and thrive, you may be really happy running it until you're ready to retire. But even then, you need some kind of plan to let yourself out. Here are some options.

You can just wind up your company. Hold a going-out-of-business sale or otherwise dispose of the intellectual property or service supports you own, and on a certain date, stop. As long as you have paid off your creditors (and depending on where you're based, perhaps some winding-up taxes), you're done. If that appeals to you, it's a simple exit strategy. In reality, however, you may have more complicated issues, like dumping loyal employees on the street, finding buyers for the things you need to dispose of, and perhaps a sense of guilt at killing off the goose that laid you all those golden eggs over the years.

Perhaps your dream for the business includes bringing in family and friends and handing it over to them. It doesn't take much imagination to recognize that this can be great, if everybody loves their roles and work as much as you hope they will. But friction, differing views of the future, possibly poorly prepared or untalented people struggling to do things they are not good at, as well as a raft of other things, can pop the balloon in a hurry. One piece of advice if you think of taking this course is to plan the transition carefully, giving people time, training and opportunities to try things on before Show Time arrives and they become the new leaders and do-ers.

You can always sell out, take on partners, or be merged, too. It can be a real eye opener when you start thinking in terms of what value your company has for another company. Maybe a firm wants access to a market, or to buyers, that you have cultivated over time. Or your products or services strategically complement theirs. Be aware, however, that many if not most of these methods of exiting may actually tie you into the company for a few more years after the sale, especially if your personal contribution—e.g., your network, some special skill or talent, or standing in the industry—is integral in your company's continued growth. And be prepared for some frustrating times within that period, because you will no longer be the big boss. You'll no doubt see approaches, visions and strategies being taken that you just don't agree with.

All this is a very high-level view of what exit strategies are all about. Whenever—or better, before—the time comes to put them into action, you'll need to learn about all your options and their implications. But the point today is that even though you are barely starting out, or you are still feeling new at the business of starting a business, an awareness of your exit options should be part of your thinking.

Hiring a Business Broker

If you want to sell your business, a well-qualified broker can make a huge difference.

SUPPOSE THE TIME HAS COME and you want to sell your business. If you're a long-term planner, you've thought about your exit strategy all along, from Day 1, and you may have cultivated one or more prospective buyers you would feel good selling to and who would value your company as you do, both emotionally and financially. In that case you may be able to sell your company yourself, with the help of your attorney and some other specialists like tax and accounting people.

But suppose that's not the case, for whatever reason. A broker is probably your best alternative. As you ponder hiring a business broker and listing your business for sale, there are a few factors that you should consider.

You obviously should hire a reputable brokerage company, but in particular, one based in your business sector. Imagine trying to sell your motel using a broker based in the gift boutique field! And aim as high as you can, in terms of the solid credibility and visibility of your broker. As with most scenarios, Big Bob's Business Brokerage Shoppe will probably deliver exactly what you think.

Ensure that you evaluate at least three brokerage firms before hiring one. Prepare a sales kit and send it to them. Then interview them, and research them via references and the press to make sure that they are reputable and have adequate experience in the field. Which companies have they sold in the last year? What process do they follow? How long does their typical sale cycle take? What are some typical sales package terms they have negotiated? Compare the three firms based on their profiles, array of services, experience, terms, and compensation. It's fair to consider whatever personal affinities you may feel with the various brokers, but be prepared to be as neutral as possible here. Your task is to sell your business, and if the broker who most matches your values and expectations for your business turns out to be a shabby huckster, you'll very much regret it later.

A serious business broker will charge you a percentage of the selling price of the business, and that percentage can vary. Some charge up front for the preparation of marketing materials. So get all of this clear in your hiring agreement, once you've made your pick—it's quite a bit like working with a real estate broker.

Before you sell, you need to find out the correct market value of your business. This will ensure that you don't undervalue your business and sell it at a loss or undervalued gain (a gain that is less than you want). You can hire an independent appraiser, or have your broker calculate the value of your business, including your business assets. The broker will probably hire an appraiser too, then ensure that all the processes are complete and see that you get all the necessary documentation for the valuation.

With your valuation complete, it's show time. Having been in the industry, experienced brokers know the best marketing techniques to use to attract and motivate buyers. It's one big reason why they can be valuable if you don't have ready-made prospects of your own. You may not end up finding any buyers if you use the wrong marketing techniques.

Apart from the valuation process and finding qualified buyers, a broker will work to get you a good deal. Successful brokers are creative, flexible, and have good marketing and negotiating skills. They also will work on your behalf to negotiate the most favorable payment and work-out agreements possible. Once an agreement is reached, they will prepare all the necessary documentation and ensure that the client makes payments as agreed.

If, after hiring a business broker, either nothing happens or you feel like you made the wrong choice, you can terminate and go with another brokerage company. However, this is subject to the contract that you have with the first broker.

So the business of selling your business is a lot like everything else you do as an entrepreneur: Survey your options, evaluate the alternatives as comprehensively as you can, and try to be objective as the process goes forward. If you succeed in this phase of your business's life, you'll have completed a full entrepreneurial cycle and—who knows?—emerge ready for the next one!

Afterword:
Where to Go from Here?

IT MAY BE SAFE TO ASSUME that if you've just finished reading this book, you are one of two types of individuals. The *curious* reader may have been interested in learning how a potentially successful business could be envisioned, created and then finally launched to compete in the marketplace. For curious readers, these pages may have even sparked your imagination about becoming an entrepreneur one day. Curious readers have always shown interest in educating and informing themselves on a new topic and enhancing their knowledgebase while doing so.

The *serious* reader may have chosen to read our book because he or she may have already decided to toss a hat in the ring and become an entrepreneur. Or perhaps, you've launched your business, and now additional tools, expert guidance, and real-world examples are vital to your success. A serious reader never stops perusing every possible source for innovative ideas, the next greatest trend, or even a leg up on the competition.

Curious or serious, we hope that everyone who has read this volume of our series found the material worthy of your time. Regardless of how or why you found us, we are glad you did.

For the guys who wrote this volume, and also founded the expertbusinessadvice.com website, the philosophy was simple:

- Create material of substance and value that can continue to be expanded indefinitely for the benefit of the reader, the customer, and the business professional
- Deliver the best possible ideas, resources and guidance to those who seek it
- Take ownership of our work, stand by it, and be proud of it

Developing this material from several points of view and delivering it to people from diverse backgrounds and with multiple levels of experience was crucial for us. In fact, it was the only way we could imagine doing it.

Simply put, our goal with this series shares the same vision as our own company's slogan: "Experts Create | We Deliver | You Apply."

The way forward begins here…

Acknowledgements

Scott wishes to thank his wife Kellin, his co-authors, his parents, the Girard Family, the Conway Family, the Edwards Family, the Seaman Family, the Warren Family (keep up the writing, Lea), the O'Keefe Family, everyone at Pinpoint Holdings Group, Barbara Stephens, Jack Chambless, Mary-Jo Tracy, Sandra McMonagle, Diane Orsini, Nathan Holic, Peter Telep, Pat Rushin, the Seminole Battalion, Dawn Price, and the Republic of Colombia (for the sweet, sweet brown nectar which fueled this project).

Mike wishes to thank his parents Tim and Gaye O'Keefe, his co-authors, Kimberly Rupert, the O'Keefe Family, the Goldsberry Family, the Roy Family, the Hubert Family, the Murat Family, the Grant Family, the Girard Family, the Price Family, the most inspiring professor Jack Chambless, his two favorite authors Clive Cussler and Timothy Ferriss, and those individuals in Argentina (for making sure there is always Malbec on the table).

Marc wishes to thank his wife Dawn, his co-authors, his mom Lynda, the Price Family, the O'Bryan Family, the Smith Family, Jean Hughes, Kellin Girard, Mike Schiano, and his life-long mentor Howard Satin.

The authors would collectively like to thank Kathe Grooms and everyone at Nova Vista Publishing, everyone at Expert Business Advice, Jon Collier, and the Van Beekum Family: Dave, Melissa and the sugar gliders.

Glossary

Accountant
One who is trained and qualified in the practice of accounting or who is in charge of public or private accounts.

Action-Centered Leadership
A type of leadership that involves leaders effectively operating remotely and negotiating the needs of the individual, team, and task within a changeable environment.

Administrative Expenses
Necessary expenses associated with the general operation of an organization that cannot be attributed to any one department or business unit.

Alpha
A coefficient which measures risk-adjusted performance, factoring in the risk due to the specific security, rather than the overall market.
Alpha personalities are dominant in groups, in contrast with Betas.

Ambition
An strong desire for some type of achievement or distinction, such as power, honor, fame, or wealth, and the willingness to strive for its attainment.

Annual Report
Audited document required by the Securities Exchange Commission in the US and sent to a public company's or mutual fund's shareholders at the end of each fiscal year, reporting the financial results for the year (including the balance sheet, income statement, cash flow statement and description of company operations) and commenting on the outlook for the future.

Backward Thinking
Thinking, commonly viewed with a negative connotation, that is typically not in sync with that of the organization or majority.

Benchmark
A standard, used for comparison.

Beta Testing	Following internal alpha testing, external beta testing can be considered a form of external user acceptance testing. Versions of a new product, known as *beta versions*, are released to a limited audience outside of the company and development team. The product is released to groups of people so that further testing can ensure the product has few faults.
Blue-Collar	A blue-collar employee is a member of the working class who usually performs manual labor. Blue-collar work may involve skilled or unskilled, manufacturing, construction, mechanical, maintenance, technical installation, and many other types of physical labor.
Bottom Line	The amount left after taxes, interest, depreciation, and other expenses are subtracted from gross sales. Also called net earnings, net income, or net profit.
Bribery	The act or practice of giving or accepting a something of value in exchange for a favor.
Brick-and-Mortar Business	A company or portion of a company with a physical presence, as opposed to one that exists only on the Internet.
Business	A commercial activity engaged in as a means of occupation or income, or an entity which engages in such activities.
Business Broker	An individual or firm who acts as an intermediary between a buyer and a business owner, typically charging a commission.
Business Ethics	The examination of the variety of problems that can arise from the business environment, and how employees, management, and the business itself can deal with them ethically.
Business Plan	A document prepared by a company's founder or management, or by a consultant on their behalf, that details the past, present, and future of the company, usually for the purpose of attracting capital investment.
Carrying Cost	The total cost of holding inventory.
Commission	A fee charged for a service in facilitating a transaction, such as the buying or selling of securities, goods or real estate.

Common Goal	The result or achievement toward which effort is directed by two or more people or organizations.
Comparative Advantage	The ability of one business entity to engage in production at a lower opportunity cost than another entity.
Compliance	The act or state of being in accordance with the relevant federal or regional authorities and their requirements.
Corporate Culture	The feel of a business; the values, atmosphere and way things are commonly done, often governed by unspoken rules and expectations. Every organization has its unique culture, whether intended or not.
Customer Service	The supply of service to customers before, during and after a purchase.
Direct Competition	When at least two people or organizations strive for a goal which cannot be shared or which is desired individually but not in sharing and cooperation.
Diversification	A portfolio strategy designed to reduce risk by combining a variety of investments, such as stocks, bonds, and real estate, which are unlikely to all move in the same direction.
Downsizing	Diminishing the total number of employees at a company through terminations, retirements, or spin-offs.
Economy	Activities related to the production and distribution of goods and services in a specific geographic region.
Empower	To give power or authority to another person or entity.
Employee	A person hired to provide services to a company on a regular basis in exchange for compensation and who does not provide these services as part of an independently owned business.
Engineer	A person trained and skilled in any of the various branches of engineering.
Entrepreneur	An individual who starts his or her own business.
Execution	A mode or style of performance.
Expansion	Growth.

Expenditure	A payment, or the guarantee of a future payment.
Favoritism	The favoring of one person or group over others with equal claims.
Financials	Documents related to finance.
Free Market	Business governed solely by the laws of supply and demand, not restrained by government interference, regulation or subsidy.
Global Marketplace	All business-related transactions that take place between two or more regions, countries and nations beyond their political boundary.
Globalization	Processes of international integration arising from increasing human connectivity and interchange of worldviews, products, ideas, and other aspects of business culture.
Goal	The result or achievement toward which effort is directed.
Graphic	A written, inscribed or drawn image.
Hierarchy	A system of persons or things ranked one above another.
Human Capital	The set of skills which an employee acquires on the job, through training and experience, and which increase that employee's value in his or her industry.
Indirect Competition	Competition among businesses that sell or produce similar products, or products that fulfill similar needs.
Industry	A basic category of corporate activity.
Insight	An instance of apprehending the true nature of a thing through intuitive understanding.
Integrity	Adherence to moral, ethical and honest principles.
Internet	Commonly called a network of networks, the Internet is a global system of interconnected computer networks that use the standard Internet protocol suite to serve billions of users worldwide.
Internet Marketing	The marketing of products or services over the Internet. Also called web marketing, online marketing, webvertising, and e-marketing.

Interview	A discussion between two people where questions are asked by the interviewer in order to gather information from the interviewee. Often part of a hiring process.
Job Description	General tasks, functions and responsibilities of a professional position.
Joint Venture	A contractual agreement joining together two or more entities for the purpose of executing a particular business undertaking.
Key Players	Individuals who have a dramatic impact on the business, decision, or operations at hand.
Lawyer	A person, licensed by the government to practice law, whose profession is to represent clients in a court of law or to advise or act for clients in other legal matters.
Lead	A suggestion that helps to direct or guide. In sales a lead is a piece of information pointing to a potential customer.
Leader	An individual who guides.
Leadership Philosophy	A standard by which leaders hold themselves and their organizations accountable for performance.
Learning Organization	Any company that facilitates the learning of its members and continuously transforms and improves itself.
Loyalty	The state or quality of staying linked to something despite options to break the link or choose alternatives.
Manager	An individual responsible for one or more areas of a business.
Manpower	The set of individuals who make up the workforce of an organization.
Market Penetration	Occurs when a business penetrates a market in which current products already exist.
Market Share	The percentage of the total sales of a given type of product or service that is won by given company.
Market Test	A geographic region or demographic group used to gauge the applicability of a product or service in a marketplace prior to a wide-scale launch.

Marketing Plan	A written document that describes the necessary actions to achieve one or more marketing objectives. It can be for a product or service, a brand, or a product line.
McGregor's Theory X	A theory of human emotion developed by Douglas McGregor that assumes that employees are inherently lazy and will avoid work if they can, and that they inherently dislike work. In response, management believes that workers need to be closely supervised and comprehensive systems of controls developed.
McGregor's Theory Y	A theory of human emotion developed by Douglas McGregor that assumes that employees may be ambitious and self-motivated and exercise self-control, and that employees enjoy their mental and physical work duties.
Micro-manage	To manage or control with excessive attention to minor details.
Middle Class	The class of people in the middle of a societal hierarchy, between the lower, working class and the upper class.
Mission Statement	A statement of the purpose of a business or organization.
Motivation	The act or an instance of encouraging actions.
Multi-Level Marketing	A sales system under which the salesperson receives a commission on his or her own sales and a smaller commission on the sales from each person he or she convinces to become a salesperson. Sometimes called pyramid marketing.
Opportunity Cost	The cost of passing up the next best choice when making a decision.
Organization	A company, business, firm, or association.
Outsourcing	Work executed for a business by people other than the business's full-time employees.
Oversight	Supervision or watchful care.
Partner	A member of a partnership, either general or limited.

Peer	A person who is equal to another in abilities, qualifications, age, background, and social or legal status.
Performance	A particular deed, action or proceeding.
Personal Factors	Factors that pertain to one's personal life that somehow impact that person's professional life.
Personal Values	An absolute or relative ethical value, the assumption of which can be the basis for ethical action.
Personnel	A body of persons employed in an organization or place of business.
Product	The end result of the manufacturing process.
Product Development	The complete process of bringing a new product to market.
Productivity	The calculated amount of output per unit of input.
Professionalism	Performing within certain standards and expectations related to character, spirit or methods.
Project	Something that is contemplated, devised or planned.
Publicly Traded Company	A company with a fixed number of shares outstanding.
Punctuality	Strict observance of time in keeping engagements.
Rapport	Relation or connection.
Result-Oriented	Focused on a result, in thought or action.
Risk/Reward	A calculated measurement of the degree of risk inherent in a given investment in relation to the potential profit associated with it.
Role	Rights, obligations and expected behavior patterns associated with a particular status.
Sales	The total amount of money collected for goods and services provided.
Sales Force	A group of people whose only corporate responsibility is to sell a company's products or services.
Sales Objectives	Targeted goals of a salesperson or sales force.
Sampling	The act or process of selecting a small but representative segment of something to test so that results can be extrapolated to a larger scale.

Search Engine Optimization (SEO)	The process of improving the popularity of a website or a web page in search engines' un-paid (*natural*) search results. In general, the earlier (or higher ranked on the search results page), and more frequently a site appears in the search results list, the more visitors it will receive from the search engine's users.
Self-Sufficient	Able to supply one's own needs without external assistance.
Selling Expenses	Costs associated with the sales process.
Selling Techniques	The body of specialized procedures and methods used by salespeople to sell goods or services.
SEO Expert	An expert in search engine optimization techniques and procedures.
Service	A type of economic activity that is intangible, is not stored, and does not result in any kind of ownership.
Shareholder	One who owns shares of stock in a corporation or mutual fund. For corporations, along with the ownership comes a right to declared dividends and the right to vote on certain company matters, including the board of directors. Also called a stockholder.
Site	See *Website*.
Slogan	A memorable motto or phrase used as a repetitive expression of an idea or purpose.
Social Media	Web-based and mobile technologies used to turn communication into interactive dialogue between organizations, communities, and individuals. Social media is ubiquitously accessible, and enabled by scalable communication techniques.
Social Networking	See *Social Media*.
Software	An accumulation of computer programs and related data that provides the instructions for telling a computer what to do and how to do it.
Stalemate	Any position or situation in which no action can be taken or progress made.

Start-up	1. The beginning of a new company or new product. 2. A new, usually small business that is just beginning its operations, especially a new business supported by venture capital and in a sector where new technologies are used.
Strategic Leadership Theory	The theory that strategic leadership provides the vision and direction for the growth and success of a business.
Strategy	A planned system of action targeting a goal or outcome.
Subordinate	Subject to, or under the authority of, a supervisor.
Superior	Higher in station, rank, degree, importance, etc.
Sustainability	The capacity to endure.
Sweatshop	Any working environment considered to be unacceptably difficult or dangerous.
SWOT Analysis	An assessment of an organization's strengths, weaknesses, opportunities and threats.
Team	A number of persons associated in some joint action.
Team Player	A person who willingly works in cooperation with others.
Technology	The branch of knowledge that deals with the creation and use of technical means and their interrelation with life, society, and the environment.
Termination	The act of coming to an end; often used to mean the end of an employee's period of employment in a given company.
Time Management	The act or process of planning and exercising conscious control over the amount of time spent on specific activities, especially to increase effectiveness, efficiency or productivity.
Trade Journal	A publication produced with the intention of target marketing to a specific industry or type of trade.
Transparency	Conditions under which facts are fully and accurately disclosed in a timely manner.

Trends	The current general direction of movement for prices or rates. Also, increasingly frequent or widespread behavior.
True Cost	The bottom-line figure when information is collected and presented for each proposed alternative. Can also mean the fully loaded cost of an item.
Unemployment Rate	Percentage of the civilian labor force which is unemployed.
Upper Level Management	A team of individuals at the highest level of organizational management who have the day-to-day responsibilities of managing a business.
Vertical Market	A market which meets the needs of a particular industry.
Web Designer	A person who plans, designs, creates and often maintains websites.
Website	A set of related web pages containing content such as text, images, video, audio, etc.
Workflow	A sequence of connected steps where each step follows the precedent without delay or gap and ends just before the subsequent step may begin.
Working Class	Those employed in lower-tier jobs.

Resources

ExpertBusinessAdvice.com

At **ExpertBusinessAdvice.com**, our goal is to become your complete resource for simple, easy-to-use business information and resources. Enjoy reading about techniques and processes necessary to develop and grow your business. **ExpertBusinessAdvice. com** offers an array of tools and resources to help you along the way by offering tutorials, downloadable templates, real-life examples, and customer support. You can even email us and a qualified member of our staff (yes, a real person!) will review your inquiry and get back to you within 24 hours. Now you can take charge of your professional growth and development, learn from others' success, and make a dramatic positive impact on your business. Learn the principles and practices that seasoned professionals use, at **ExpertBusinessAdvice.com,** for free!

THE WAY FORWARD BEGINS HERE...

Want to learn how to start a business? Are you looking for an additional income stream? No problem—we can get you started down the right path. Do you want to know how to plan, creating the necessary documents to obtain financing for your business? Maybe you just want to learn how experienced business leaders streamline financial models, maximize output, inspire managers, and incentivize employees, tapping the full range of resources available. Regardless of your needs, **ExpertBusinessAdvice. com** is here for you!

www.expertbusinessadvice.com

CRASH COURSE for ENTREPRENEURS

Many novice entrepreneurs have little more than a brilliant idea and a pocketful of ambition. They want to know *Now what?* This 12-title series tells *exactly what you must know*, in simple terms, using real-world examples. Each two-hour read walks you through a key aspect of being an entrepreneur and gives practical, seasoned, reader-friendly advice.

Whether your dream business is dog walking or high-tech invention, home-based or web-based, these books will save you time and trouble as you set up and run your new company. Collectively, these three young Florida-based serial entrepreneurs have successfully started seventeen new companies across a broad range of sectors and frameworks, including finance, international sourcing, medical products, innovative dot-com initiatives, and traditional brick-and-mortar companies.

A Crash Course for Entrepreneurs—From Expert Business Advice

Starting a Business – Everything you need to build a new business, starting from scratch.

Sales and Marketing – Solid guidance on successfully developing and promoting your business and its brand.

Managing Your Business – Proven techniques in managing employees and guiding your business in the right direction.

Business Finance Basics – Tax tips, funding, money management, basic accounting, and more!

Business Law Basics – A must-know overview on types of businesses, risks and liabilities, required documents, regulatory requirements, and the role of a business attorney. *Co-Author: Mark R. Moon, Esq.*

Franchising – A how-to guide for buying and running a franchise business.

Business Plans - Perhaps the most important thing you can do to get your start-up off to a great start is to create a strong business plan. Here's how!

Time and Efficiency – Wheel-spinning is the most destructive force in business. Make the most of your time to maximize income and motivate employees.

International Business – The world is a big place filled with billions of potential partners and customers. This guide offers tips to reach them all.

Supplemental Income – Can't commit full time? No problem! Here's how to make extra money in your spare time.

Social Media – This rapidly-growing networking and advertising medium is changing the world. Here's how to use it to grow your business.

Web-Based Business – The biggest, most valuable companies out there today are Internet businesses. Here's why, and how you can build one yourself.

Paperback and eBook format available. 160 pages, 6 ½" × 9" (16.5 × 23 cm), US$16.99, with extensive glossary and index.

Index

Tip: We suggest that you check the Glossary (pages 135-144) for definitions related to terms you want to look up in this index.

About the Authors

Scott L. Girard, Jr.

Editor-in-Chief, Expert Business Advice, LLC
Email: scott@expertbusinessadvice.com

Before joining Expert Business Advice, Scott was Executive Vice President of Pinpoint Holdings Group, Inc., where he directed multiple marketing and advertising initiatives. Scott was a key player for the Group, negotiating and facilitating the sourcing logistics for the commercial lighting industry division, which supplied clients such as Gaylord Palms, Ritz Carlton, Marriott, Mohegan Sun, and Isle of Capri with large-scale lighting solutions. His vision and work were also pivotal in the growth and development of Bracemasters International, LLC.

Scott has degrees in Business Administration and English Writing and is a published contributor to various periodicals on the topics of economics and politics. He is also a co-author and series editor of *A Crash Course for Entrepreneurs* book series. A graduate of the United States Army Officer Candidate School, Scott is a combat veteran, having served a tour in Kuwait and Iraq as an infantry platoon leader in support of Operation Iraqi Freedom and Operation New Dawn.

Originally from Glendale, California, Scott now lives in St. Petersburg, Florida with his wife. Scott is a regular contributor to www.expertbusinessadvice.com. His side projects include a collection of fiction short stories and scripts for two feature films. His motto: "Words have meaning."

Michael F. O'Keefe

Chief Executive Officer, Expert Business Advice, LLC
Email: mike@expertbusinessadvice.com

In 2004, Mike founded O'Keefe Motor Sports, Inc. (OMS Superstore), eventually growing it into the largest database of aftermarket automotive components available for online purchase in the world. Currently, aside from his position at Expert

Business Advice, LLC, Mike is President of Pinpoint Holdings Group, Inc. and Vice President of Marketing for Bracemasters International, LLC.

At Pinpoint, Mike's focus is building a strong base for understanding the global marketplace. He also plays a key role in facilitating the logistics of the commercial lighting branch of the company, bridging between Pinpoint's office in Wuxi, China, and their commercial clients—hotel chains such as Gaylord Palms, Ritz Carlton, Marriott, Mohegan Sun and Isle of Capri.

Recently, Mike's passion and talents for cutting-edge business techniques and practices have led to the exponential growth of Bracemasters. By developing web-based marketing strategies and E-commerce initiatives, as well as formatting on-line documents that enabled the company to reach a vast number of current and potential patient-customers, Mike increased Bracemasters' website viewership by 17,000% in two years.

Originally from Delavan, Wisconsin, Mike now lives in Orlando, Florida. He is a regular contributor to www.expertbusinessadvice.com. His motto: "Rome did not create a great empire by having meetings; they did it by killing all those who opposed them."

Marc A. Price

Director of Operations, Expert Business Advice, LLC
Email: marc@expertbusinessadvice.com

Marc has collaborated with the Federal Government, United States Military, major non-profit organizations, and some of the largest corporations in America, developing and implementing new products, services and educational programs. Equally skilled in Business-to-Business and Business-to-Consumer functions, Marc has facilitated product positioning, branding and outreach efforts on many different platforms for the organizations he has worked with.

As an entrepreneur, Marc has successfully directed the launch of seven different companies, ranging from traditional brick-and-mortar establishments to innovative dot-com initiatives. Four were entertainment production companies (sound, lighting, staging, logistics, talent, entertainment), one was a business services company serving small companies, one was concerned with business and land acquisition, and two were website and business consulting services. Using his expertise in organizational management and small business development, Marc's latest focus is on working with new entrepreneurs and small-to-medium-sized businesses in emerging industries.

As an accomplished public speaker and writer, Marc has appeared on nationally syndicated television and radio networks, in national print publications, and has been the subject of numerous interviews and special-interest stories. Marc is a regular contributor to www.expertbusinessadvice.com.

Marc received his Bachelor of Science in Organizational Management from Ashford University. He and his wife divide time between Orlando, Florida and elsewhere, including an active schedule of international travel. His motto: "You can't build a reputation on what you are going to do."—Henry Ford

Business Efficiency Resources

Get More Done Seminars

Grooms Consulting Group, a sister company to Nova Vista Publishing, offers proven training that saves professionals one month or more of time wasted on email, information and meeting inefficiency.

• 83% of all professionals are overloaded by email – we can save up to 3 weeks a year, per person
• 92% want to improve their information storage system – we can make searches 25% faster and more successful
• 43% of all meeting time is wasted – we can save up to another 3 weeks per year, per person

"We saved 15 days a year!"
Matt Koch, Director of Productivity
Capital One Financial Services

Three Two-Hour Modules: We offer three powerful seminars: **Get Control of Email**, **Get Control of Info**, and **Get Control of Meetings**.
They can be delivered in any combination you wish and can be customized.
Who Should Attend? Anyone who handles email, stores information, and attends meetings. Leaders leverage their position for added impact.
Delivery Options: Seminar, keynote speech, webinar, e-learning, and executive coaching.
Return on Investment (ROI): We can measure the impact of every session on participants with five-minute online pre- and post-surveys. We deliver a report that shows time saved, productivity gained, participant satisfaction, and other significant impacts.

Special pricing is available for groups.

Three Get More Done Modules: Combine and Customize as You Wish

1. GET CONTROL OF EMAIL
• Pump up your productivity by eliminating unnecessary email
• De-clutter your jammed inbox
• Write more effective messages
• Discover time-saving Outlook® / Lotus® tech tips
• Improve email etiquette and reduce legal liability
• Choose the best communication tool

2. GET CONTROL OF INFORMATION
• Get organized, once and for all
• Never lose a document again
• File and find your information in a flash; make shared drives productive
• Make better decisions with the right information
• Create an ordered, stress-free folder structure throughout your system

3. GET CONTROL OF MEETINGS
• Meet less and do more through virtual and other advanced options
• Reduce costs, boost productivity and go green with improved, efficient virtual meetings
• Run engaging, productive live meetings
• Discover time-saving e-calendar tips
• Keep every meeting productive and on track, make follow-ups easy

Satisfaction Guaranteed
We guarantee that the vast majority of your people will rate our seminars "excellent" or "good", or your money back.

"A huge hit with our people!"
Joel Burkholder
Regional Program Coordinator – ACLCP

Contact: Kathe Grooms
kgrooms@groomsgroup.com

Two Must-Read Books For Entrepreneurs

Time Out for Leaders: Daily Inspiration for Maximum Leadership Impact

Donald Luce and Brian McDermott

Leaders around the world recognize that daily reflection is absolutely necessary for defining values, establishing direction and pursuing vision. Luce and McDermott, two of the world's leading international consultants in leadership development, help leaders take ten minutes a day to focus on the principles they live by and help those around them develop and prosper.

In an attractive page-a-day format, each workday features a pithy quote, a reflection, and an action. A great gift for leaders you know, and for the leader in you.

"It is lonely at the top. Leaders can benefit from a daily dose of courage and values in Time Out for Leaders *and then approach their demanding tasks with renewed energy."*

Rosabeth Moss Kanter, Harvard Business School

Time Out for Leaders (ISBN for hardcover 978-9077256-10-7, ISBN for softcover 978-90-77256-30-6)
272 pages, 145 × 190 mm (5 ½" × 7")
Suggested retail price €19.95. $19.95 hardcover; €14.95, $14.95 softcover
Quote-a-day format; hardcover is jacketed with marker ribbon.

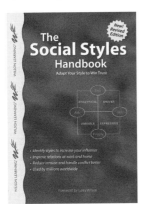

Social Styles Handbook: Adapt Your Style to Win Trust

Backed by a database of more than 2 million people, Wilson Learning's Social Styles concepts are powerful, life-changing communication tools. The ways people prefer to influence others and how they feel about showing emotion identify them as Analyticals, Expressives, Drivers or Amiables. You feel comfortable acting within your own style. But to relate to others well, you must consciously adjust your style to theirs. That's Versatility, which improves performance in every aspect of your work and life.

Find your style and learn to recognize others'. Understand and appreciate the strengths and differences in each. Learn how to become Versatile while still being yourself. Important tools for recognizing tension and Back-Up Behavior and handling it productively, plus techniques for influencing others, have made this a best-selling book that delivers results.

"I'm not sure I can quantify the value of using Social Styles, but I know I would not want to do my job without it."

Ann Horner, Main Board Director, Bourne Leisure Limited

Social Styles Handbook (ISBN Revised Edition 978-90-77256-33-6)
192 pages, softcover, 160 × 230 cm (6" × 9")
Suggested retail price: € 19.95, US$19.95
Models, charts, anecdotes, an index and other resources.

Now available in eBook formats!
www.novavistapub.com

CAREERS
I Just Love My Job!
Roy Calvert, Brian Durkin, Eugenio Grandi and Kevin Martin, in the Quarto Consulting Library (ISBN 978-90-77256-02-2, softcover, 192 pages, $19.95)

Taking Charge of Your Career
Leigh Bailey (ISBN 978-90-77256-13-8, softcover, 96 pages, $14.95)

LEADERSHIP AND INNOVATION
Grown-Up Leadership
Leigh Bailey and Maureen Bailey (ISBN 978-90-77256-09-1, softcover, 144 pages, $18.95)

Grown-Up Leadership Workbook
Leigh Bailey (ISBN 978-90-77256-15-2, softcover, 96 pages, $14.95)

Leading Innovation
Brian McDermott and Gerry Sexton (ISBN 978-90-77256-05-3, softcover, 160 pages, $18.95)

SALES
Win-Win Selling
Wilson Learning Library (ISBN 978-90-77256-34-3, softcover, 160 pages, $18.95)

Versatile Selling
Wilson Learning Library (ISBN 978-90-77256-03-2, softcover, 160 pages, $18.95)

Time Out for Salespeople
Nova Vista Publishing's Best Practices Editors, (ISBN 978-90-77256-14-5 hardcover with marker ribbon, 272 pages, $19.95; ISBN 978-90-77256-31-2 softcover, 272 pages, $14.95)

Get-Real Selling, Revised Edition
Michael Boland and Keith Hawk (ISBN 978-90-77256-32-9, softcover, 144 pages, $18.95)

SCIENCE PARKS, ECONOMICS, ECOLOGY OF INNOVATION
What Makes Silicon Valley Tick?
Tapan Munroe, Ph.D., with Mark Westwind, MPA (ISBN 978-90-77256-28-2, softcover, 192 pages, $19.95)

**Visit www.novavistapub.com for sample chapters, reviews, links and ordering.
eBooks are now available too!**